READING
EXPLORER

NANCY DOUGLAS • DAVID BOHLKE

Second Edition

Australia • Brazil • Japan • Korea • Mexico • Singapore • Spain • United Kingdom • United States

Reading Explorer 1
Second Edition

Nancy Douglas and David Bohlke

Publisher: Andrew Robinson

Executive Editor: Sean Bermingham

Senior Development Editor: Derek Mackrell

Associate Development Editor:
  Ridhima Thakral

Director of Global Marketing: Ian Martin

Product Marketing Manager: Lindsey Miller

Senior Content Project Manager: Tan Jin Hock

Manufacturing Planner: Mary Beth Hennebury

Compositor: Page 2, LLC.

Cover/Text Design: Creative Director:
  Christopher Roy, Art Director: Scott Baker,
  Designer: Alex Dull

Cover Photo: O. Louis Mazzatenta/
  National Geographic Creative

Student Book with Online Workbook:
ISBN-13: 978-1-305-25452-7

Student Book:
ISBN-13: 978-1-285-84685-9

National Geographic Learning
20 Channel Center Street
Boston, MA 02210
USA

Cengage Learning is a leading provider of customized learning solutions with office locations around the globe, including Singapore, the United Kingdom, Australia, Mexico, Brazil, and Japan. Locate your local office at:
international.cengage.com/region

Cengage Learning products are represented in Canada by Nelson Education, Ltd.

Visit National Geographic Learning online at **NGL.Cengage.com**

Visit our corporate website at **www.cengage.com**

Printed in the United States
7 8 9 10 11 — 23 22 21 20 19

Contents

Scope and Sequence

Unit	Theme	Reading
1	**Amazing Animals**	**A:** The Incredible Dolphin **B:** Musical Elephants
2	**Travel and Adventure**	**A:** The Trip of a Lifetime **B:** Adventure Island
3	**The Power of Music**	**A:** Hip-Hop Planet **B:** A Musical Boost
4	**Into Space**	**A:** Life Beyond Earth? **B:** Living in Space
5	**City Life**	**A:** Global Cities **B:** Rio Reborn
6	**Small Worlds**	**A:** In One Cubic Foot **B:** A World Within Us
7	**When Dinosaurs Ruled**	**A:** The Truth about Dinosaurs **B:** Mystery of the Terrible Hand
8	**Stories and Storytellers**	**A:** The Brothers Grimm **B:** The Tale of the Seven Ravens
9	**Unusual Jobs**	**A:** Meet the Meteorite Hunter **B:** Smokejumpers
10	**Uncovering the Past**	**A:** The Army's True Colors **B:** Wonders of Egypt
11	**Legends of the Sea**	**A:** Pirates: Romance and Reality **B:** Women of the Waves
12	**Vanished!**	**A:** Mystery on Everest **B:** The Missing Pilot

Reading Skill	Vocabulary Building	Video
A: Understanding the Gist **B:** Identifying Main Ideas in Paragraphs	**A:** Word Link: *-ance / -ence* **B:** Word Link: *-ist*	Monkey College
A: Understanding Maps **B:** Finding Key Details	**A:** Usage: *record* **B:** Word Partnership: *native*	Land Divers
A: Classifying Information **B:** Identifying Reasons (1)	**A:** Usage: *female* **B:** Word Link: *-ation / -ion*	Steel Drums
A: Summarizing Using a Concept Map **B:** Identifying Reasons (2)	**A:** Word Partnership: *message* **B:** Word Link: *in- / im-*	Women in Space
A: Understanding Charts and Graphs **B:** Understanding a Writer's Use of Quotes	**A:** Word Link: *inter-* **B:** Word Partnership: *separate*	High-Rise Challenge
A: Understanding Sequence **B:** Understanding Pros and Cons	**A:** Word Partnership: *environment* **B:** Word Link: *-ful / -less*	Under Yellowstone
A: Supporting Ideas with Examples **B:** Using Definitions to Find Meaning	**A:** Word Link: *-er / -or* **B:** Word Partnership: *opinion*	Dinosaur Discovery
A: Annotating Text **B:** Understanding Pronoun Reference	**A:** Word Link: *en-* **B:** Usage: *effect / affect*	Sleepy Hollow
A: Identifying Exact vs. Approximate Numbers **B:** Paraphrasing Sentences	**A:** Word Link: *il- / ir-* **B:** Word Link: *-ment*	Wildfire Photographer
A: Identifying Homonyms **B:** Creating an Outline Summary	**A:** Word Partnership: *reveal* **B:** Word Partnership: *task*	Peru's Hidden Treasure
A: Finding Similarities and Differences **B:** Using Context to Guess the Meaning of Words	**A:** Word Link: *-dom* **B:** Word Link: *trans-*	Blackbeard's Cannons
A: Arguing For and Against a Topic **B:** Identifying Transition Words	**A:** Word Link: *-ever* **B:** Word Link: *dis-*	Earhart Mystery

Welcome to Reading Explorer!

In this book, you'll travel the globe, explore different cultures, and discover new ways of looking at the world. You'll also become a better reader!

What's new in the Second Edition?

New and updated topics

Explore the power of music, the world's top global cities, and life inside the human body.

New Reading Skill section

Learn how to read strategically—and think critically as you read.

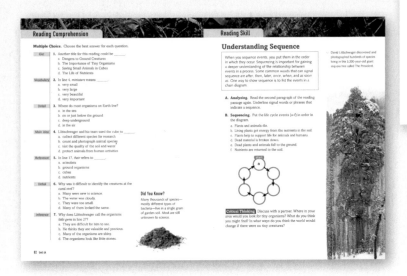

Expanded Viewing section

Apply your language skills when you watch a specially adapted National Geographic video.

Now you're ready
to explore your world!

AMAZING ANIMALS

An orangutan swings from a tree in Kabili-Sepilok Forest Reserve, Malaysia.

Warm Up

Discuss these questions with a partner.

1. What are some things humans can do that animals can't?

2. What are some things animals can do that humans can't?

3. Which is your favorite animal? Why?

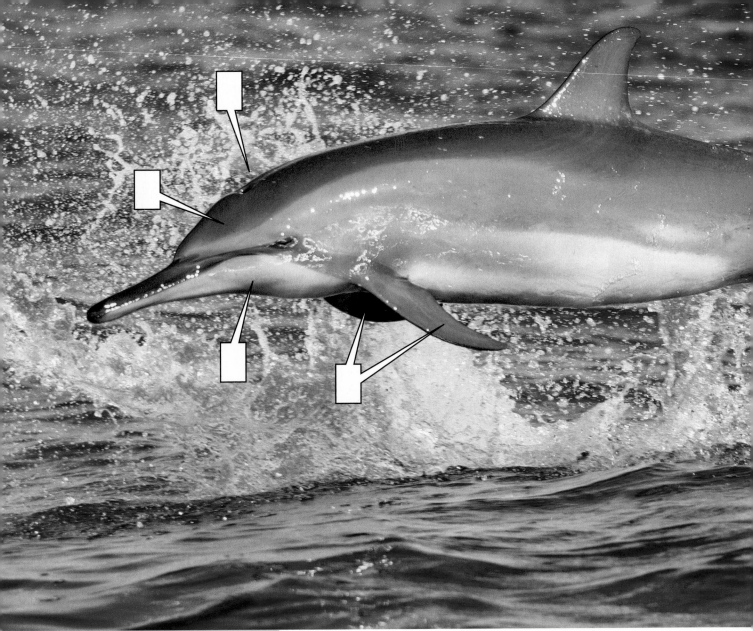

Before You Read

A bottlenose dolphin leaps above the water.

A. Labeling. Match each description (1–5) with the correct part of the dolphin.

1. Dolphins sleep by resting one half of their **brain** at a time.
2. A dolphin's **tail** doesn't have any bones, but it is full of muscles. These help to push the dolphin through the water.
3. Dolphins "hear" through a special bone in their lower **jaw**.
4. The bones inside a dolphin's **flippers** are similar to the bones inside your arm and hand.
5. Dolphins are mammals, not fish. They breathe air using a special hole (called a **blowhole**) on the top of their head.

B. Skimming. On the next two pages, look at the title, headings, photos, and captions. What is the reading about? Circle **a**, **b**, or **c**. Then read the passage to check your answer.

a. types of dolphins   b. things dolphins do   c. what dolphins eat

THE INCREDIBLE DOLPHIN

1 Many people say dolphins are **intelligent**. They seem to be able to think, understand, and learn things quickly. But are they as **smart** as humans, or are they more like cats and dogs? Dolphins use their brains quite differently from the way humans do. But scientists say dolphins and humans are **alike** in some ways. How?

5 ## Communication

Like humans, every dolphin has its own "name." The name is a special whistle.[1] Each dolphin chooses a **specific** whistle for itself, usually by its first birthday. Dolphins are like people in other ways, too. They "talk" to each other about a lot of things—such as their age, their feelings, and finding food. They also use a
10 **system** of sounds and body language to communicate. Understanding dolphin **conversation** is not easy for humans. No one "speaks dolphin" yet, but some scientists are trying to learn.

---

1 A **whistle** is a high-pitched sound made by blowing air through a hole.

Play

15 Dolphins are also social animals. They live in groups called *pods*, and they often join others from different pods to play games and have fun—just like people. Scientists believe playing together is something only intelligent animals do.

Teamwork

20 Dolphins and humans are similar in another way: both species make plans for getting things they want. In the seas of southern Brazil, for example, dolphins use an intelligent **strategy** to get food. When there are fish near a boat, dolphins signal[2] to the fishermen to put
25 their nets in the water. Using this **method**, the men can catch a lot of fish. Why do dolphins **assist** the men? There is an **advantage** for them: they get to eat some of the fish that escape from the net.

---

2 If you **signal** to someone, you make an action or a sound to tell that person something.

Dolphins sometimes help fishermen find food.

Dolphins travel together in groups known as pods.

Reading Comprehension

Multiple Choice. Choose the best answer for each question.

Main Idea

1. What does the reading NOT mention?
   a. how dolphins communicate with each other
   b. how dolphins play games and have fun
   c. how dolphins work together as a team
   d. how dolphins move quickly through the water

Detail

2. Where does a dolphin get its "name"?
   a. It gets it from its mother.
   b. It gets it from scientists.
   c. It chooses it for itself.
   d. No one knows.

Detail

3. Which sentence about dolphin language is true?
   a. Dolphins "talk" to each other about many things.
   b. Dolphins whistle, but they don't use body language.
   c. Dolphin conversation is easy for humans to understand.
   d. Dolphins don't "talk" about their feelings.

Detail

4. Which sentence about dolphins and humans is NOT true?
   a. Dolphins and humans use their brains in the same way.
   b. Dolphins and humans play games in groups.
   c. Dolphins and humans plan ways to do things.
   d. Dolphins and humans communicate their feelings
      to each other.

Reference

5. In line 15, *others* refers to other _____.
   a. pods
   b. people
   c. dolphins
   d. games

Detail

6. Why do dolphins sometimes help fishermen?
   a. Dolphins are kind animals.
   b. The dolphins can get food that way.
   c. The dolphins are scared of humans.
   d. The fishermen ask the dolphins for help.

Vocabulary

7. In the sentence *They get to eat some of the fish . . .*
   (lines 27–28), what does *get to* mean?
   a. are able to
   b. have to
   c. should
   d. want to

Did You Know?
The orca, or killer whale, is actually a kind of dolphin.

Understanding the Gist

The **gist** of a text is what the text is mainly about. When you read for the gist, don't read every word. Skim the text quickly to find out what it is basically about. Look at the title and any headings, photos, and captions. Another strategy is to read the first line of each paragraph.

A. Multiple Choice. Skim the passage on pages 9–10 again. What is the main idea of the reading? Circle **a**, **b**, or **c**.

   a. Some types of dolphins are much smarter than humans.

   b. Scientists believe there are many different types of dolphins.

   c. Dolphins are intelligent and, in some ways, are like humans.

B. Multiple Choice. Skim this short passage and answer the questions (1–2) below. Then read the passage again and check your answers.

> The albatross is one of the world's largest flying birds. It also has the largest wings of any bird—up to 3.4 meters (slightly over 11 feet) from tip to tip. These giant birds use their wings to ride the ocean winds. They can fly for hours without rest, or even without moving their wings. Some may even be able to sleep while flying.
>
> Most albatrosses spend nearly all their time in the air. In fact, they only return to land to breed.[1] A parent albatross might fly thousands of kilometers to find food for its young. In its lifetime, an albatross can fly a total of more than six million kilometers (3.8 million miles).

1 When animals **breed**, they produce young.

1. What is the above passage mainly about?

   a. where albatrosses live

   b. albatross flying behavior

   c. albatross intelligence

2. What could be a title for this passage?

   a. Riding the Ocean Winds

   b. Catching Fish

   c. The Smartest Bird

Critical Thinking Discuss with a partner. The reading on pages 9–10 mentions three ways to tell if an animal is intelligent. What are they? Can you think of other ways to tell if an animal is intelligent?

∧ A wandering albatross

Vocabulary Practice

A. Matching. Read the information below and match each word in **red** with its definition.

There are a few ways to test how **smart** animals are. One **method** is to test memory. Scientists in Japan showed a group of college students and a group of five-year-old chimps the numbers 1 to 9 in different places on a computer screen. The test was to see if the groups could remember the **specific** position of the numbers in the correct order. Every time, the chimps were faster than the students. Why? Did someone **assist** the chimps? No, but the animals probably had an important **advantage**: They were young. As both humans and animals get older, their memory gets worse.

1. _____: a way of doing something

2. _____: help

3. _____: something that helps you succeed

4. _____: exact

5. _____: intelligent

∧ A Sumatran orangutan, *Pongo abelii*

B. Completion. Complete the information with the words and phrases from the box.

| alike | conversation | intelligent | language system | strategy |

Orangutans and humans are **1.** _____ in some ways. For example, did you know that the orangutan is a very **2.** _____ animal? Orangutans use a(n) **3.** _____ to stay dry when it rains: They take leaves from trees and use them like umbrellas. These animals don't have a complex[1] **4.** _____ like humans do. But today, some orangutans are learning basic sign language. Maybe, in the future, we will be able to have a simple **5.** _____ with them.

1 If something is **complex**, it is made up of many parts.

> **Word Link** The suffixes **-ance** and **-ence** at the end of a word indicate that it is a noun. For example, *assistance* is the noun form of *assist*. It means "helping someone."

Elephant musicians in Lampang, Thailand

Before You Read

A. Labeling. Read the information and label the parts of the picture (1–5).

Can an (**1**) **elephant** make music? Some people might say "no," but the animals in this photo are musicians. Each elephant uses its (**2**) **trunk** to play different (**3**) **instruments** such as the (**4**) **drum** or the (**5**) **xylophone**.

B. Predict. Which of these things do you think elephants can do? Check (✓) your answer(s). Then read the information on the next page to see if your prediction(s) are correct.

☐ dance   ☐ paint   ☐ cook food

MUSICAL ELEPHANTS

MYANMAR (BURMA) · Lampang · LAOS · THAILAND · Bangkok · CAMBODIA · Gulf of Thailand · MALAYSIA

ASIA · THAILAND · INDIAN OCEAN

1   In the town of Lampang in northern Thailand, there is an unusual[1] group of musicians. They play many different kinds of music—from traditional Thai songs to music by Beethoven. Both children and adults love this group. What makes them so
5   **popular**? Is it their music? Their looks?[2] Yes, it's both of these things, but it's also something else: they're elephants.

These musical elephants are from the Thai Elephant Conservation Center (TECC) in Lampang. The TECC protects elephants. It teaches people to understand and care for these
10 **huge**, but **gentle**, animals. And, like many zoos around the world, the TECC **encourages** elephants to paint.

Richard Lair works with the TECC. He knew that elephants hear better than they see. So he had an idea: if elephants are intelligent and they have good hearing, maybe they can
15 play music. To test his idea, Lair and a friend started the Thai Elephant Orchestra.[3] During a **performance**, the elephants play a variety of instruments, including the drums and the xylophone. The animals also use their voices and trunks to make sounds.

But can elephants really make music **properly**? Yes, says Lair.
20 They're very **creative**. Humans may encourage the animals to play instruments, but the elephants make their own songs; they don't just copy their **trainers**
25 or other people. There are now CDs of the group's music, which **earn** money for the TECC. And the music these **artists** create is pretty amazing.

---

1 If something is **unusual**, it does not happen very often or you do not see it or hear it very often.

2 When you refer to someone's **looks**, you are referring to how beautiful or ugly they are.

3 An **orchestra** is a large group of musicians that play a variety of instruments together.

Reading Comprehension

Multiple Choice. Choose the best answer for each question.

Gist

1. Another title for this reading could be _____.
   a. Teaching Elephants to Paint
   b. Elephants in Danger
   c. TECC Trainers
   d. An Unusual Orchestra

Detail

2. The elephants at the TECC _____.
   a. see better than they hear
   b. are encouraged to paint
   c. cannot create their own music
   d. make their own instruments

Reference

3. In line 4, *them* refers to _____.
   a. children
   b. adults
   c. songs
   d. musicians

Detail

4. Why did Richard Lair start the Thai Elephant Orchestra?
   a. He had heard the elephants playing music.
   b. He needed to make money for the TECC.
   c. He believed elephants could play music.
   d. He wanted to be on TV in Thailand.

Vocabulary

5. In line 17, what does *a variety of* mean?
   a. the same kind of
   b. many different
   c. two types of
   d. too many

Detail

6. Which sentence about the Thai Elephant Orchestra is
   NOT true?
   a. The elephants dance while playing music.
   b. The elephants use their trunks to make sounds.
   c. The elephants use their voices to make sounds.
   d. The orchestra's CD sales earn money for the TECC.

Paraphrase

7. Read the last sentence in the passage again. What does
   it mean?
   a. The elephants play great music.
   b. Human artists now play with the elephants.
   c. The elephants are very beautiful.
   d. Human musicians want to copy the elephants' songs.

Did You Know?

In south Asia, an elephant's trainer is known as a *mahout* [ma-**hoot**]. Here, a mahout in Sri Lanka is brushing the teeth of his elephant.

Identifying Main Ideas in Paragraphs

A paragraph usually has one main idea and some details that support it. Paragraphs often include a topic sentence that describes the main idea. Usually—but not always—a topic sentence is at or near the start of the paragraph, or at the end of the paragraph. One way to find the main idea quickly is to read the sentences at the beginning and end of the paragraph. A paragraph's heading (if it has one) can also give a clue to its main idea.

A. Multiple Choice. Read the paragraph. Which sentence gives the main idea? Circle **a**, **b**, or **c**.

In 2005, a dog named Bella met an elephant named Tarra at a conservation center. Dogs and elephants don't usually mix, but this pair soon became best friends. One day, workers heard Bella barking from the room where she was resting. She was communicating with Tarra, who was outside making noises of her own. So someone brought Bella outside to Tarra, who gently touched her friend with her trunk. Over the years, the two animals often slept and had food together. When Bella died in 2011, Tarra carried her body to a place where they often spent time together.

△ Bella and Tarra

a. In 2005, a dog named Bella met an elephant named Tarra at a conservation center.

b. Dogs and elephants don't usually mix, but this pair soon became best friends.

c. When Bella died in 2011, Tarra carried her body to a place where they often spent time together.

B. Matching. What is the main idea of each paragraph in the reading on page 15? Match each main idea below to a paragraph (1–4). One idea is extra.

1. _____   a. Richard Lair created the Thai Elephant Orchestra.
2. _____   b. There is an unusual group of musicians in Thailand.
3. _____   c. Animals all over the world like music.
4. _____   d. Elephants really can play amazing music.
                e. The TECC works with elephants.

Critical Thinking Discuss with a partner. Which animal do you think is the smartest in this unit? Why do you think so?

A. Words in Context. Complete each sentence with the correct answer (**a** or **b**).

1. A **gentle** person _____ hurt an animal.

    a. wouldn't   b. would

2. A **huge** animal is very _____.

    a. large   b. small

3. If something is **popular**, _____ people like it.

    a. a lot of   b. very few

4. If you do something **properly**, you do it _____.

    a. poorly   b. correctly

5. An example of a musical **performance** is _____.

    a. an orchestra playing music   b. someone learning to play an instrument

B. Completion. Complete the paragraph with words from the box. One word is extra.

artists	creative	earn	encourage	popular	trainers

In some zoos, **1.** _____ show elephants how to hold a paintbrush.
The trainers **2.** _____ the elephants to choose colors and use them
to make paintings. Of course, not every painting is good. Just like humans, only
some elephants are very **3.** _____. Now, an online gallery sells
paintings by these elephant **4.** _____. By doing this, the gallery
hopes to **5.** _____ money to protect elephants.

< This painting, called "Green Symphony," was painted by Phong, an elephant at the Lampang Elephant Art Academy.

Word Link We can add **-ist** to words to form nouns. These nouns often describe jobs, such as *artist* and *scientist*.

Courtesy of NOVICA.COM

VIEWING Monkey College

Before You Watch

A. Labeling. Label the numbered items in the photo with the words in **bold** from the caption.

∧ A **trainer** in Thailand is teaching a **monkey** how to pick a **coconut**. He ties a **rope** around it and uses this to control and direct the animal up a **tree**.

1. _____

2. _____

3. _____

4. _____

5. _____

B. Matching. How do you think the trainer trains the monkey? Number the steps in order from 1 to 4.

_____ The trainer lets the monkey play.

_____ The trainer lets the monkey pick a coconut.

_____ The trainer shows the monkey how to spin a coconut.

_____ The trainer encourages the monkey to spin a coconut himself.

While You Watch

A. Checking. Check your answers to **B** on page 19. Did you guess the steps correctly?

B. Completion. Complete the word web about the video. Use verbs from the box. Two words are extra.

buy	earn	fall	have	pick	produce	spin	treat	use	work

How to Train

- show how to **1.** _____ a coconut
- encourage the monkey to do it himself
- let the monkey **2.** _____ a coconut

Advantages

- if people climb trees, they might **3.** _____ and die

Training Monkeys

Importance of Coconuts

- people **4.** _____ them on beaches
- used in curry
- farmers can **5.** _____ money

Life of Monkeys

- farmers say most **6.** _____ a good life
- some people make them **7.** _____ too hard
- farmers will continue to **8.** _____ them

After You Watch

Critical Thinking. Discuss these questions with a partner.

1. What else do you think monkeys can be trained to do?

2. Do you think it's a good idea to train monkeys to help humans? Why or why not?

3. Which other animals help humans? How?

This pig-tailed Macaque ❯ (Macaca nemestrina) is trained to pick coconuts.

TRAVEL AND ADVENTURE

A cyclist enjoys the view from a rock ledge near Delores, Colorado.

Warm Up

Discuss these questions with a partner.

1. When you travel, what kinds of activities do you like to do?

2. What places in the world would you most like to visit? Why?

3. What is the most adventurous trip you have been on?

Before You Read

A. Scan. Look at the map and read the information below. Answer these questions.

    1. Where did the two friends travel from and to? How did they travel?

    2. How far did they travel? How long did the journey take?

B. Discussion. Why do you think they wanted to make this trip?

CYCLING THE AMERICAS

In 2005, Gregg Bleakney, with his friend Brooks Allen, began an amazing two-year cycling adventure.

Route ●

Starting point: Prudhoe Bay, Alaska

End point: Ushuaia, Argentina

Total distance: 30,500 kilometers (19,000 miles)

Source: National Geographic Maps

START
Prudhoe Bay, AL

San Francisco, CA

Mexico City, Mexico

Panama City, Panama

La Paz, Bolivia

FINISH — Ushuaia, Argentina

THE TRIP OF A LIFETIME

1   Many people dream of going on a great travel adventure. Most of us keep dreaming; others make it happen.

Gregg Bleakney's dream was to travel the Americas from top to bottom. He got the idea after he finished a 1,600-kilometer (1,000-mile)
5   bike ride. Gregg's friend, Brooks Allen, was also a cyclist. The two friends talked and decided their **goal**: they would travel from Alaska to Argentina—by bike.

To pay for the **journey**, Gregg and Brooks worked and saved money for years. Once they were on
10   the road, they often camped outdoors or stayed in hostels.[1] In many places along their **route**, local people opened their homes to the two friends and gave them food.

---

1   A **hostel** is a cheap place to stay and sleep when traveling.

In Guatemala, Brooks Allen and Gregg Bleakney cycled through Tikal National Park.

Lessons from the Road

15 During their trip, Gregg and Brooks cycled through deserts, rainforests, and mountains. They visited **modern** cities and explored **ancient** ruins[2] such as Tikal in Guatemala. In many places, they met other cyclists from all over the world.

In May 2007—two years, twelve countries, and over 30,500 km
20 (19,000 miles) later—Gregg **eventually** reached Ushuaia, Argentina, at the tip of South America. (Near Guatemala, Brooks had to return to the U.S. and Gregg continued without him.)

Gregg and Brooks kept a **record** of their adventures in an online blog. The trip taught both men a lot about traveling. Here is some of
25 Gregg's **advice**:

Travel light. The less baggage you have, the less you'll worry about.

Be flexible. Don't plan everything. Then you'll be more **relaxed** and happy, even when there are **challenges** along the way.

Be polite. As one traveller told Gregg, "Always remember
30 that nobody wants to fight, cheat, or rob[3] a nice guy."

---

2 The **ruins** of something are the parts that remain after it is damaged or weakened.

3 If someone **robs** you, they take money or property from you.

⌄ End of the Road: Ushuaia, Argentina—the world's southernmost city

Reading Comprehension

Multiple Choice. Choose the best answer for each question.

Gist

1. What could be another title for the reading?
   a. Cycling from Alaska to Argentina
   b. The Southernmost City in the World
   c. Things to Do and See in America
   d. Argentina: The Land of Adventure

Detail

2. Which sentence about the trip is NOT true?
   a. To pay for the trip, they saved money and traveled cheaply on the road.
   b. Only Gregg made the complete trip from Alaska to Argentina.
   c. During their trip, Gregg and Brooks met people from all over the world.
   d. In Guatemala, Gregg got sick and went back to the U.S.

Reference

3. In line 13, *them* means _____.
   a. the local people
   b. Gregg and Brooks
   c. other cyclists
   d. their friends

Sequencing

4. What happened after Brooks returned to the U.S.?
   a. Gregg went on a 1,600 kilometer bike ride.
   b. Gregg continued to the south of Argentina.
   c. Gregg traveled through Mexico City.
   d. Gregg visited Tikal National Park.

Vocabulary

5. In line 26, what does *baggage* mean?
   a. things you take on a trip
   b. places you visit on a trip
   c. plans you make for a trip
   d. reasons for going on a trip

Paraphrase

6. What does Gregg mean by "*Be flexible*" in line 27?
   a. Be ready to change easily.
   b. Be careful when you travel.
   c. Plan the details of your trip
   d. Choose an easy way to travel.

Inference

7. Which statement would Gregg most likely agree with?
   a. In other countries, only stay in hotels or with people you know.
   b. Plan every part of your trip. Then you'll be happier.
   c. When abroad, learn how to say "thank you" in the local language.
   d. Bring a lot of things on your trip so you don't have to buy anything.

Did You Know?

In Prudhoe Bay, Alaska, the sun does not set from mid-May through mid-July.

Reading Skill

Understanding Maps

Like other visuals, maps can help you better understand a text. Most maps have a **title**, a **scale** (to show distance in real life), a **key** or **legend** (a guide of symbols used), and a **source** (where the information comes from). A map may also include a **compass** (to show where north is). Also look for how colors are used.

A. Labeling. Look at the map below. Label the parts of the map with the features (1–4).

1. key
2. source
3. scale
4. title

Spread of H5N1 Virus Around the World

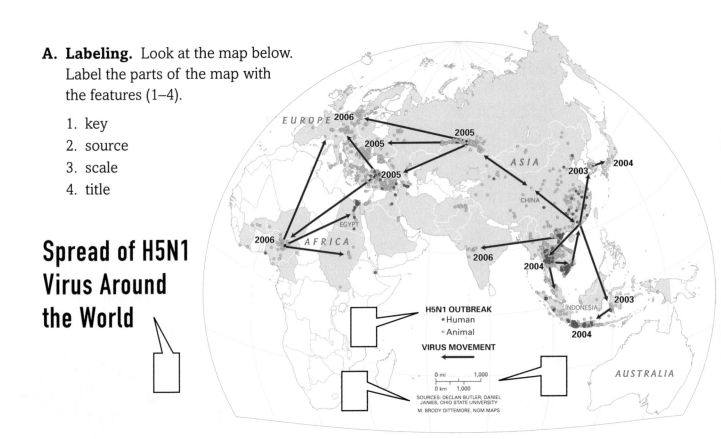

EUROPE 2006
2005
2005
2005
ASIA
2003
2004
CHINA
EGYPT
2006 AFRICA
2006
2004
2003
INDONESIA
2004
AUSTRALIA

H5N1 OUTBREAK
• Human
• Animal

VIRUS MOVEMENT

0 mi   1,000
0 km   1,000

SOURCES: DECLAN BUTLER; DANIEL JANIES, OHIO STATE UNIVERSITY
M. BRODY DITTEMORE, NGM MAPS

B. Completion. What does the map above show? Circle the correct word in parentheses to complete each sentence.

1. The H5N1 virus, or "bird flu," started in (**Asia / Africa**) in 2003.

2. The virus moved (**east / west**) in 2005.

3. There are (**fewer / more**) human H5N1 cases than animal H5N1 cases.

4. The virus traveled the farthest in (**2004 / 2005**).

Critical Thinking From the map on page 22, which parts of the journey do you think were the most challenging for the cyclists? Why?

Vocabulary Practice

A. Words in Context. Complete each sentence with the correct answer (**a** or **b**).

1. If something is **ancient**, it is very _____.
   a. expensive   b. old
2. Which of these is a **modern** invention?
   a. the cell phone   b. paper
3. A **record** of an event will help you _____ it.
   a. change   b. remember
4. If something is a **challenge**, it is _____ to do.
   a. difficult   b. easy

B. Completion. Complete the information using words from the box.

advice	eventually	goals	journey	relax	route

Every year, many people make mistakes when they go hiking. Here's some **1.** _____ that can help you stay safe:

Before you start your **2.** _____, leave a map showing the **3.** _____ that you are planning to take. If something goes wrong (for example, if you get lost or hurt), you should "S.T.O.P." This means:

   Stop: try to **4.** _____ and stay calm.

   Think about your situation.

   Observe: look around and notice where you are.

   Plan what to do next: decide on one or two simple **5.** _____.

It's also important to stay in one place. Someone will **6.** _____ look for you.

> **Usage** *Record* is a noun; the stress is on the first syllable: **rec**ord. *Record* is also a verb; the stress is on the second syllable: re**cord**.

⌃ A lost hiker plans a new route

Vanuatu is a popular tourist spot in the South Pacific, where tourists can enjoy a variety of extreme sports and activities. One of the most popular activities is volcano trekking at Mount Yasur (pictured above).

Before You Read

A. Discussion. Read the caption. Then answer the questions below.

1. Why do you think extreme sports and activities are popular?

2. What is the most extreme sport or activity you have tried?

B. Predict. Look at the title and headings on the next page. What do you think these activities are like? Check your ideas as you read.

ADVENTURE ISLAND

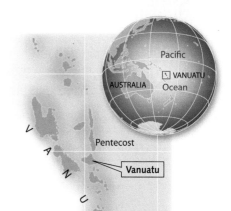

1 Vanuatu is a **nation** of small islands in the South Pacific. It is one of the smallest countries in the world. But for those interested in adventure and sport, there is a lot to do. Some of the best swimming, snorkeling, and sea kayaking can be found here. Vanuatu's islands also offer visitors two of the
5 most exciting—and dangerous—activities in the world: volcano surfing and land diving.

Volcano Surfing

On Tanna Island, Mount Yasur rises 300 meters (1,000 feet) into the sky. Yasur is one of a few active volcanoes in the country. It erupts[1] almost
10 every day, sometimes several times a day. For **centuries**, both island locals and visitors have climbed this mountain to visit the top. Recently, people have also started climbing Yasur to surf the volcano. In some ways, volcano surfing is like surfing in the sea, but in other ways, it's very different. A volcano surfer's goal is to **escape** the erupting volcano—without being **hit**
15 by flying rocks! It's fast, fun, and dangerous—the perfect **extreme** sport.

Land Diving

Most people are **familiar** with bungee jumping. But did you know bungee jumping started on Pentecost Island in Vanuatu, and is almost 15 centuries old? The original activity, called land diving, is part of a **religious**
20 ceremony.[2] A man **ties** tree vines[3] around his ankles. He then jumps headfirst from a high tower. The goal is to touch the earth with the top of his head—without breaking the vine or hitting the ground hard. Every spring, island **natives** (men only) still perform this amazing test of **bravery**.

---

1 When a volcano **erupts**, it throws out hot rock called lava.
2 A **ceremony** is a formal event, such as a wedding.
3 A **vine** is a plant that grows up or over things.

Reading Comprehension

Multiple Choice. Choose the best answer for each question.

Purpose

1. What is the purpose of this reading?
   a. to encourage people not to do dangerous sports
   b. to explain what volcano surfing and land diving are
   c. to talk about the world's best volcano surfer and land diver
   d. to compare Vanuatu with other islands in the South Pacific

Reference

2. In line 2, what does *those* refer to?
   a. people
   b. countries
   c. activities
   d. islands

Detail

3. Which sentence about Vanuatu is NOT true?
   a. It is a small nation in the South Pacific.
   b. It is where bungee jumping began.
   c. It has more than one active volcano.
   d. It is famous for a sport called volcano diving.

Detail

4. Which sentence is true about Mount Yasur?
   a. It is no longer active.
   b. It is more than 1,000 meters high.
   c. People have been climbing it for a long time.
   d. It's on Pentecost Island.

Detail

5. Which sentence is true about land diving?
   a. It was first called "bungee jumping."
   b. It came to Vanuatu from another country.
   c. It is less popular today than in the past.
   d. It is a traditional activity in Vanuatu.

Vocabulary

6. In line 21, what does *the earth* mean?
   a. the people
   b. the ground
   c. the tower
   d. the world

Main Idea

7. How are volcano surfing and land diving similar?
   a. They are both old sports.
   b. Both men and women do them.
   c. They are both done on Tanna Island.
   d. They are both extreme activities.

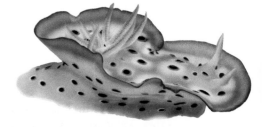

Did You Know?

Vanuatu is also a popular destination for scuba divers. Underwater creatures there include extremely colorful sea slugs like the one above.

Finding Key Details

To answer questions about a text, you often need to find specific details. Before you read, you first need to decide what to look for, for example, a person's name, a place, or a number. Once you know what to look for, scan the text quickly to find that information.

A. Multiple Choice. Read the questions. What kind of answer will you need to scan for? Circle **a**, **b**, or **c**. (Do not answer the questions yet.)

1. Where can you surf with sharks?
   a. a place   b. a number   c. a date

2. How high are the highest waves on the "silver dragon"?
   a. an example   b. a number   c. a reason

3. Why is surfing possible in so many places?
   a. a reason   b. a place   c. an example

4. What other hobby is popular among surfers?
   a. a place   b. a reason   c. an activity

∧ Surfers at China's Qiantang river

B. Completion. Now scan the text below and write answers to the questions above.

1. _____   2. _____

3. _____   4. _____

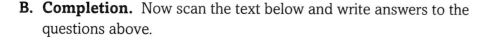

When you think of surfing, you probably think of Hawaii, Australia, or Brazil. But surfers don't need warm weather, or even an ocean. For example, some surfers ride the waves—and see the sharks—in the cold waters off South Africa. Some even surf in icy Antarctica. Other surfers head to China's Qiantang River to surf the "silver dragon." Twice a year, the waves on the Qiantang can reach a height of ten meters (33 feet).

Surfing is possible in all these places because all a surfer needs is a wave and a board. There is always a risk, so surfers need to be strong swimmers. They also need good balance and an ability to think and move quickly. This is why skateboarding is a common hobby among surfers.

Critical Thinking Discuss with a partner. How is surfing on water similar to volcano surfing? How is it different?

Vocabulary Practice

A. Definitions. Complete the definitions using words from the box. One word is extra.

escape	extreme	familiar	nation	native	religious

1. If you _____ from something, you run away from it.
2. A(n) _____ is a country.
3. A(n) _____ of somewhere is from that place.
4. If you are _____ with something, you know or understand it well.
5. If you are _____, you believe in a god or gods and you follow a set of rules or beliefs.

B. Completion. Circle the correct word in parentheses to complete the information below.

The festival of San Fermin in northern Spain is famous for "the running of the bulls." Hundreds of people run in front of a group of bulls. Runners wear white; they also **1. (escape / tie)** a red scarf around their bodies. The run lasts three minutes. Runners try to **2. (hit / escape)** from the bulls without falling or getting **3. (tie / hit)** by them.

Running with the bulls started in Spain in the 13th **4. (century / nation)**, and it is still very popular today. Pamplona **5. (nations / natives)** and visitors from many **6. (nations / extremes)** around the world join in. The run is very dangerous. So why do people do it? For some runners, it is a test of **7. (bravery / familiarity)**. For others, the run makes them feel alive.

> **Word Partnership** Use *native* with nouns: native **country**, native **land**, native **language**, native **tongue**.

∧ People wearing red and white run from the bulls in Pamplona, Spain.

VIEWING Land Divers

Before You Watch

A. True or False? What do you remember about land diving from the reading on page 29? Read the sentences. Circle **T** for *true* and **F** for *false*.

1. It happens on Pentecost Island in Vanuatu.   **T**   **F**

2. It is about five centuries old.   **T**   **F**

3. Only men do it.   **T**   **F**

B. Matching. Match these captions (a–d) to the correct photos (1–4).

a. For the first time, a small camera is tied to a diver's leg.
b. Land divers jump from a 21-meter-high (68.9 feet) tower.
c. A diver's friends help free him from the vines around his ankles.
d. A diver's goal is to touch the earth with the top of his head.

1. ☐

2. ☐

3. ☐

4. ☐

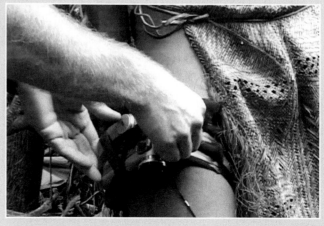

While You Watch

A. Noticing. Check (✓) all of the dives that are shown.

- ☐ **1.** a dive into water
- ☐ **2.** a dive that doesn't go well
- ☐ **3.** a dive with a camera tied to a leg
- ☐ **4.** a dive that goes well
- ☐ **5.** a dive when someone dies
- ☐ **6.** a dive by a Western man

B. Words in Context. Circle the correct answers.

1. *Naghol* means _____.

    a. land diving   b. ancient event

2. The tower is built _____.

    a. in a jungle   b. next to a town

3. While at the tower, if you have second thoughts, you must _____.

    a. not jump   b. close your eyes

4. People _____ every year.

    a. die   b. get hurt

5. People from abroad _____ jump.

    a. can   b. cannot

After You Watch

Critical Thinking. Discuss these questions in a group.

1. Would you ever land dive? Why or why not?

2. Do you think more or fewer people will do land diving in the future? Why?

3. How do people in your country show bravery?

∧ A land diver leaps from a tower at Londot Village, Pentecost Island.

THE POWER OF MUSIC

An audience cheers as a concert begins.

Warm Up

Discuss these questions with a partner.

1. What is your favorite kind of music? Who is your favorite artist or group?

2. Does your country have any well-known types of music or musicians?

3. How do certain types of music make you feel? Give some examples.

Before You Read

A. Matching. Read the information and match each word in **bold** with its definition.

Rap and hip-hop may seem like very modern types of music. But did you know they actually have long histories going back hundreds of years? The origins of rap and hip-hop go back more than 400 years. In West Africa, storytellers called *griots* used spoken words and music to tell stories, usually over the beat of drums. In the 17th century, many African people were brought to America as slaves—people who are treated as property and made to work. They used these musical traditions to sing about their **hardships**. Even after the end of slavery, spoken-word music continued to be an important part of their **culture**. It was later used by the first rap and hip-hop artists in the late 1970s. Today, rap and hip-hop are popular not just among U.S. **teenagers** but with people all over the world.

1. _____ : the ideas, customs, and social behavior of a particular group of people

2. _____ : people from 13 to 19 years old

3. _____ : things that are difficult in life

B. Skimming. On the next two pages, look at the title, headings, and first paragraph. What is the passage mainly about? Circle **a**, **b**, or **c**. Then read the passage to check your answer.

    a. famous hip-hop artists   b. the history of hip-hop   c. hip-hop in two countries

HIP-HOP PLANET

Trillectro Festival at the Half Street Fairgrounds in Washington, D.C.

1   Hip-hop started in New York City in the 1970s but has become popular all over the world. Today, many countries have their own local hip-hop scenes.[1] Artists from different **backgrounds** rap about everything from cars and designer clothes to social **issues**. Here are two examples.

The Czech Republic

Europe is home to 10–12 million Roma—a group of people often called "gypsies." Many Roma are poor. In some places, they also face discrimination.[2]

Now some Roma teenagers are using hip-hop to teach tolerance.[3] In the Czech Republic, Roma teens meet for a hip-hop class called "Rap for **Peace** Hip-Hop." Their instructor is Shameema Williams. She is a member of the all-**female** rap group Godessa, from South Africa.

In the lessons, the teens learn to write rap music and use it to teach others about Roma culture. These teens, Williams believes, can use music to change their lives and other people's **attitudes**.

---

1 You can refer to an area of activity as a **scene**, for example, an art or a music scene.
2 If you **face discrimination**, you are treated less fairly or less well than others.
3 **Tolerance** means accepting different people, religions, beliefs, and so on.

Dakar, Senegal

Assane N'Diaye loves hip-hop music. He grew up in a small fishing village in Senegal. For a time, he was popular as a DJ in **clubs** in Dakar, the capital city of Senegal.

20　Today, N'Diaye lives in his village again. He formed a rap group with other family members. They rap about their lives as village fishermen and about working long, hard days and earning almost no money. Many people in their **audience** can understand these things.

25　"Rap," N'Diaye says, "doesn't **belong** to American culture. It belongs here. It has always existed here, because of our pain and our hardships . . ."

N'Diaye **dreams of** having a better life. He wants to make a CD and help his family. **Despite** his hardships, the music gives
30　N'Diaye hope.

A modern-day griot, or storyteller, performs with another musician on a beach in Senegal.

Reading Comprehension

Multiple Choice. Choose the best answer for each question.

Purpose

1. What is the purpose of this reading?
   a. to compare American and African rap music
   b. to say why some people do not like rap music
   c. to describe different hip-hop scenes
   d. to explain how hip-hop started

Detail

2. Who is Shameema Williams?
   a. a Senegalese singer
   b. a Roma teenager
   c. a Czech musician
   d. a South African rapper

Did You Know?

Some people think the word rap comes from "rhythm and poetry." In fact, the word was used in the 1960s to mean "talk." Later, in the 1970s, it was used to refer to a type of music.

Vocabulary

3. In line 11, what does the word *instructor* mean?
   a. DJ
   b. classmate
   c. member
   d. teacher

Detail

4. Which sentence about the Roma teenagers is NOT true?
   a. They are using music to teach people about their culture.
   b. In some places, they are disliked because they are Roma.
   c. They are taking a hip-hop class.
   d. Most of them are from South Africa.

Detail

5. Which statement about Assane N'Diaye is true?
   a. His music is about his life as a DJ.
   b. He is going to move to the United States.
   c. He has already made several CDs.
   d. He lives in a small village.

Inference

6. Which statement would Assane N'Diaye most likely agree with?
   a. The best rappers are from the United States.
   b. Rap music is a part of Senegal.
   c. Rap music came to Africa recently.
   d. Many Africans don't understand rap music.

∧ A DJ spinning turntables

Reference

7. In the sentence *It belongs here* (line 26), *it* refers to _____.
   a. rap
   b. hardship
   c. American culture
   d. pain

Classifying Information

As you read, think about how the information and ideas are connected. Does the information relate to a single topic? Can you group—or classify—the ideas based on their similarities or differences?

A. Classification. Look back at the passage on pages 37–38. Complete the Venn diagram by matching each statement (a–e) with the person it describes.

  a. helps students write rap music
  b. raps about life in a small village
  c. was a DJ
  d. is a member of a South African rap group
  e. believes rap music can make life better

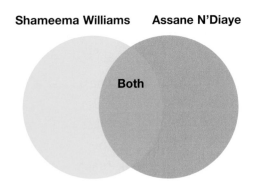

Shameema Williams   Assane N'Diaye

Both

B. Classification. Read the following passage and classify the information using the chart below.

The modern history of hip-hop can be divided into two periods: Old School and New School. Old School hip-hop refers to the early days of the music, starting from the late-1970s to the mid-1980s. The music was influenced by disco and funk music of the 1970s. Old School hip-hop is also known for its simple rapping style compared to the style of hip-hop that followed. New School hip-hop started in the mid-1980s and lasted until the late 1990s. This period saw the birth of many different hip-hop styles, influenced by genres such as rock 'n' roll, and soul music. The music was often serious and angry, with lyrics that focused on social and political issues.

	Old School	New School
Time period		
Influences		
Style of music		

Vocabulary Practice

A. Completion. Complete the information below using the correct forms of the words in **red**.

> Hip-hop started on the streets and in the **clubs** of New York City. **Despite** this, hip-hop's look and sound don't **belong** to the United States alone. The music changes everywhere you go. A person from one **background**—for example, a Moroccan man living in Paris—might rap about one thing. But another person—for example, a **female** musician from Los Angeles—will rap about something different.

1. Shameema Williams is a _____ rap artist.
2. If something _____ to you, you own it.
3. _____ are places where you can listen to music and dance.
4. Your _____ is information about you—where you come from, your religion, and so on.
5. _____ being a recent form of music, hip-hop is very popular worldwide.

> **Usage** *Female* is commonly used as an adjective, but it is sometimes used as a noun; in everyday conversation, *women* is usually more polite than *females*.

B. Completion. Complete the information using the correct forms of words from the box.

attitude	audience	background	dream of	issue	peace

The Palestinian group DAM raps in several languages, including English and Arabic. The group's members come from different
1. _____, and their music focuses on different social
2. _____. For example, they sing about the problems of women and young people. They also talk about the need for
3. _____ and tolerance. The members of DAM
4. _____ changing people's 5. _____—
they want to help people think differently about certain things.
Today, the group performs for 6. _____ in many countries.

Critical Thinking Discuss with a partner. Shameema Williams believes music can change people's attitudes. Do you agree with her? Why or why not?

Before You Read

A. Discussion. Look at the images and caption on this page. Discuss answers to the following questions with a partner.

1. Which part(s) of the brain do you use when you sing? Play an instrument? Listen to music?

2. In what ways do you think music and language are similar?

B. Skimming. On the next page, read the title and the headings. Answer the questions below. Then read the passage to check your answers.

1. The word *boost* in the title probably means _____.
   a. improvement
   b. problem
   c. system

2. What do you think is the main idea of the reading?
   a. The brain can be trained to be more musical.
   b. People with musical training are more successful.
   c. Music can help the brain in many ways.

△ When we sing, listen to music, or play an instrument (such as the violin), we use many different parts of our brain—for example, areas for listening, speaking, memory, movement, and emotion.

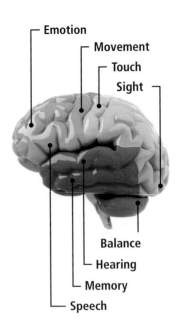

Emotion
Movement
Touch
Sight
Balance
Hearing
Memory
Speech

A MUSICAL BOOST

1 Is there a **connection** between music and language? According to recent studies, the answer is yes: music boosts certain language abilities in the brain. Here, we look at two examples.

Music and Hearing

5 A recent study by researcher Nina Kraus shows that playing a musical instrument can improve a person's hearing ability. As a part of the study, two groups of people listened to a person talking in a noisy room. The people in the first group were musicians, while those in the second group had no musical training. The musicians were able to hear the talking
10 person more clearly.

Musicians hear better, says Kraus, because they learn to pay attention to **certain** sounds. Think about violinists in an orchestra. When the violinists play with the group, they hear their own instrument and many others, too. But the violinists must listen closely to what they are playing, and
15 **ignore** the other sounds. In this way, musicians are able to **concentrate** on certain sounds, even in a room with lots of noise.

Music and Speaking

Gottfried Schlaug, a doctor at Harvard Medical School, works with stroke[1] patients. Because of their illness, these people cannot say their
20 names, addresses, or other information **normally**. However, they can still sing. Dr. Schlaug was surprised to find that singing words helped his patients to eventually speak. Why does this work? Schlaug isn't sure. Music seems to activate[2] different parts of the brain, including the **damaged** parts. This somehow helps patients to use that part of the
25 brain again.

Understanding the Results

Music **improves** concentration, memory, listening **skills**, and our **overall** language abilities. It can even help sick people get better. Playing an instrument or singing, says Nina Kraus, can help us do better in school
30 and keep our brain **sharp** as we get older. Music, she adds, is not only enjoyable, it's also good for us in many other ways.

---

1 A **stroke** is an illness of the brain. It can make a person unable to move one side of his or her body. A stroke sometimes damages (hurts) the parts of the brain used for language.
2 To **activate** something is to make it work.

Reading Comprehension

Multiple Choice. Choose the best answer for each question.

Gist

1. Another title for the Music and Hearing section could be _____.
   a. Trained to Listen
   b. How to Be a Musician
   c. Playing in an Orchestra
   d. The Power of Music

Detail

2. What two groups did Nina Kraus study?
   a. noisy people and quiet people
   b. musicians and non-musicians
   c. violinists and other musicians
   d. people with hearing problems and people without hearing problems

Vocabulary

3. What does *pay attention to* mean in line 11?
   a. enjoy
   b. make
   c. listen for
   d. look for

Detail

4. What is true about both Nina Kraus and Gottfried Schlaug?
   a. They are both medical doctors.
   b. They both work at Harvard Medical School.
   c. They both play an instrument in an orchestra.
   d. They are both interested in how music and the brain are connected.

Did You Know?

According to scientists, music study helps to improve teamwork skills and discipline.

Reference

5. In line 13, what does *they* refer to?
   a. orchestra musicians
   b. instruments
   c. violinists
   d. the sounds of the orchestra

Detail

6. How does Gottfried Schlaug help stroke patients speak?
   a. by repeating their name and address
   b. by playing music for them
   c. by asking them to sing words
   d. by getting them to play an instrument

Detail

7. Which type of improvement is NOT mentioned in the reading?
   a. memory
   b. school grades
   c. language ability
   d. sleep

Identifying Reasons (1)

A reading text may contain one or more reasons why an action happens. Identifying *why* things happen helps you better understand the relationship between actions in the text. The reason may come before or after the action or effect. Words that signal reasons include *because (of)*, *since*, and *due to*. In the following examples, the reason is underlined:

Musicians hear better because <u>they learn to pay attention to certain sounds</u>.

Singing words may help stroke patients since <u>it activates a different part of the brain</u>.

Because of <u>this need to concentrate</u>, musicians hear many sounds better.

A. Identifying. Read the passage below. Circle the words that signal reasons.

How has Western music reached every corner of the world? Researchers believe Western music is popular because of its ability to express emotions across cultures.

Cameroon

Researcher Thomas Fritz played parts of 42 Western songs to members of the Mafa, an ethnic group in Cameroon. Since he wanted to include a variety of Western music types, Fritz played classical, rock, pop, and jazz. He asked the group members to point to pictures of people's faces to show the emotion the music expressed.

The Mafa were able to identify the emotions correctly. This was probably due to the fact that the rhythms and melodies of Western music are similar to the emotional features of human speech.

B. Completion. Complete the sentences with the correct reasons from the passage.

1. Researchers believe Western music is popular _____

   _____.

2. Thomas Fritz played classical, rock, pop, and jazz _____

   _____.

3. The Mafa probably identified the emotions correctly _____

   _____.

Critical Thinking Discuss with a partner. Have you ever used music to help you study or to help you learn something? How did music help?

Vocabulary Practice

A. Words in Context. Complete each sentence with the correct answer.

1. If you **ignore** something, you _____ it.
   a. don't pay attention to   b. focus on

2. A **certain** sound refers to _____.
   a. only one type of sound   b. any type of sound

3. If you **concentrate**, you _____.
   a. think very hard   b. don't think at all

4. Two examples of **skills** are _____.
   a. food and drink   b. reading and writing

5. A person's **overall** abilities means his or her abilities _____.
   a. related to a single skill   b. as a whole

B. Completion. Complete the information using the correct forms of words from the box. One word is extra.

connection	damaged	ignore	improve	normally	sharp

In his book *Musicophilia*, brain scientist Dr. Oliver Sacks looks at the **1.** _____ between music and the brain. He writes about how music **2.** _____ the lives of musicians, hospital patients, and ordinary people.

Dr. Sacks also shares the experiences of different people. He gives an example of a man whose brain was **3.** _____ by a lightning strike, which left him wishing to become a musician at age 42. He also gives an example of people who listen to an orchestra, but hear only noise. The most interesting example, however, is of a man whose memory **4.** _____ lasts only seven seconds, except when he listens to music. When this happens, his mind becomes very **5.** _____, with a near-perfect memory.

△ Dr. Oliver Sacks

Word Link We can add **-ation** and **-ion** to some verbs to form nouns (for example, *inform + -ation = information*; *connect + -ion = connection*). These nouns describe an action or a state of being.

VIEWING Steel Drums

Before You Watch

A. Matching. You will hear these words in the video. Match them to their definitions.

1. steel (*n.*) •
2. tune (*v.*) •
3. oil (*n.*) •
4. ban (*v.*) •
5. beat (*v.*) •
6. invent (*v.*) •

• a. to make or create something for the first time
• b. a thick liquid used as a fuel
• c. to state that something must not be done
• d. to hit a musical instrument to make a sound
• e. a strong metal used to make many products
• f. to make changes to a musical instrument so it produces the right notes

B. Discussion. Look at the photos and read the captions. How do you think steel drums are made? Discuss with a partner.

∧ An oil drum is a large container that holds oil.　　∧ A man carries an old oil drum.

∧ A steel drum is a musical instrument.

While You Watch

A. Matching. Check (✓) the topics that are discussed.

☐ where steelband music comes from   ☐ steelband in modern Africa

☐ the popularity of steelband music   ☐ steelband's place in local culture

☐ steelband music's relationship to Africa   ☐ international steelband musicians

B. Matching. Who says these things? Match the person to what he or she says.

1. Tony ☐   **2.** Beverly ☐   **3.** Dove ☐

a. "Well, it's the music of my country, so . . . I should learn it. I should know a little bit about it."

b. "Pan is most important to Trinidad and Tobago. It's part of our culture. It was invented in Trinidad and Tobago."

c. "Pan is to Trinidad part of our main culture. This is ours. We made it, we created it."

After You Watch

A. Inferring. Most steelband musicians play music "by ear." What do you think this means?

B. Critical Thinking. Making steel drums from old oil drums is an example of "upcycling"— the process of making new products from waste products. Look at these items and discuss with a partner ways you might upcycle them.

a glass water bottle   **a wire hanger**   **a paint can**

a rubber tire   **candy wrappers**   **an old computer**

4

INTO SPACE

The Space Shuttle *Endeavour* lights up the sky as it leaves the Kennedy Space Center in Florida, U.S.A.

Warm Up

Discuss these questions with a partner.

1. Have you seen a movie or TV show about space? Describe it.

2. Do you think life exists on other planets? Why or why not?

3. Do you think governments should spend money on space

Before You Read

A. Matching. Read the information and match each word in **bold** with its definition.

The Kepler Space **Telescope** is named after Johannes Kepler, a German **astronomer** from the 17th century. It was sent off into **space** in 2009 to study 170,000 stars in a small and distant part of our **galaxy**. Since then, the Kepler Space Telescope has discovered over a hundred **planets** and identified nearly 3,000 more objects that could be planets, including a few that may have life.

1. _____ is everywhere beyond the Earth.
2. Mars, Venus, Jupiter, and Earth are all _____.
3. A(n) _____, such as our own Milky Way, is a group of stars, gas, and dust.
4. A(n) _____ is someone who studies stars and other objects in space.
5. A(n) _____ is an instrument designed to make distant objects appear closer. It is commonly used to look out into space.

B. Skim. Read the first paragraph on the next page. Answer the question below. Then read the whole passage to check your ideas.

What do Shostak and Barnett think?

    a. We might soon communicate with beings from space.

    b. We will probably never find intelligent life outside Earth.

    c. We have probably already contacted beings from space.

LIFE BEYOND EARTH?

A view of the Carina Nebula taken by the Hubble Space Telescope. The nebula is about 6,500 light years from Earth, and contains some of the largest and brightest stars in our galaxy.

1 Is there intelligent life on other planets? For years, scientists said "No" or "We don't know." But today, this is changing. Seth Shostak and Alexandra Barnett are astronomers. They believe intelligent life exists somewhere in the universe.[1] They also think we will soon **contact**
5 these beings.[2]

Why do Shostak and Barnett think intelligent life exists on other planets? The first reason is time. Scientists believe the universe is about 12 billion years old. This is too long, say Shostak and Barnett, for only one planet in the **entire** universe to have intelligent life. The
10 second reason is size—the universe is huge. **Tools** such as the Hubble Telescope "have shown that there are at least 100 billion . . . galaxies," says Shostak. And our galaxy, the Milky Way, has at least 100 billion stars. Some planets that **circle** these stars might be similar to Earth.

---

1 The **universe** is all of space—all stars, planets, and other objects.
2 A person or a living creature (for example, an animal) is a **being**.

Looking for Intelligent Life

15　Until recently, it was difficult to **search for** signs of intelligent life in the universe. But now, **powerful** telescopes **allow** scientists to **identify** many more small planets—the size of Mars or Earth—in other solar systems. If these planets are similar to Earth, they might have intelligent life.

Making Contact

20　Have beings from space already visited Earth? Probably not, says Shostak. The **distance** between planets is too great. Despite this, intelligent beings might eventually contact us using other methods such as radio signals.[3] In fact, they could be trying to communicate with us now, but we may not have the right tools to receive their **messages**. But this is changing, says
25　Shostak. Within the next 20 years, we could make contact with other life forms in our universe.

3　A **radio signal** is a way of sending information using radio waves.

< Scientists are hoping to build rockets that could reach the closest stars.

Reading Comprehension

Multiple Choice. Choose the best answer for each question.

Purpose

1. What is the main purpose of this reading?
 a. to explain how life started on Earth
 b. to explain why we might find intelligent life outside of Earth
 c. to show how telescopes work
 d. to describe what life on other planets might look like

Main Idea

2. What could be another title for the last paragraph?
 a. When Aliens Visited Earth
 b. The Distance Between Planets
 c. Our Galaxy: The Milky Way
 d. Communicating with Intelligent Life

Detail

3. Which reason for the existence of intelligent life is NOT mentioned?
 a. There are planets in other solar systems that might be the size of Earth.
 b. Some planets that circle stars might be similar to Earth.
 c. The universe is too old to have just one planet with intelligent life.
 d. Some other planets in the Milky Way have water.

Detail

4. What kinds of planets are most likely to have intelligent life?
 a. Earth-size planets in our solar system
 b. Earth-size planets in other solar systems
 c. larger planets in our solar system
 d. larger planets in other solar systems

Detail

5. Why doesn't Shostak think intelligent beings have visited Earth?
 a. They are waiting for us to contact them.
 b. They don't have enough knowledge about Earth.
 c. They are waiting for our technology to improve.
 d. The distance to Earth is too great.

Did You Know?

In April 2013, the Kepler Space Telescope found two Earthlike planets that might have water and—maybe— intelligent life.

Reference

6. In lines 25–26, what does *life forms* refer to?
 a. messages
 b. radio signals
 c. beings
 d. planets

Detail

7. Why does Shostak think we may make contact with intelligent life within the next 20 years?
 a. We will have better technology to receive their messages.
 b. We will be better able to send radio signals.
 c. Bigger telescopes will identify an Earthlike planet.
 d. Intelligent life will finally receive messages that we sent to them.

Summarizing Using a Concept Map

When you summarize, you record the main ideas and key details of a text. A concept map can help you illustrate these ideas in a clear and logical way, and it can help you organize and understand information better. In a concept map, the main ideas or concepts of the text are linked by words and phrases that explain the connection between the ideas.

You can build a concept map by first starting with a main idea, topic, or issue to focus on. Then note the key concepts that link to this main idea. The bigger and more general concepts come first, which are then linked to smaller, more specific concepts. Use linking phrases and words to connect the concepts.

A. Analyzing. Look back at the reading on pages 51–52. Discuss with a partner the kind of information you will need in order to summarize the text. Underline the main ideas and key details in the text.

B. Summary. Complete the concept map below with words from the reading.

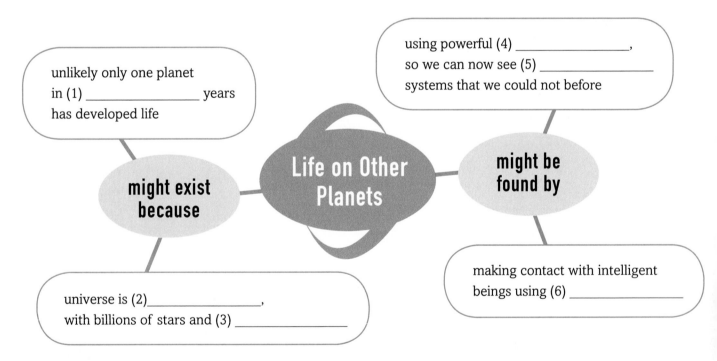

unlikely only one planet
in (1) _____ years
has developed life

using powerful (4) _____,
so we can now see (5) _____
systems that we could not before

might exist because

Life on Other Planets

might be found by

universe is (2)_____,
with billions of stars and (3) _____

making contact with intelligent
beings using (6) _____

Critical Thinking Discuss with a partner. What other reasons can you think of that life on other planets might or might not exist?

Vocabulary Practice

A. Completion. Complete the sentences by circling the correct word or phrase in each pair.

Does life exist on other planets? Scientists use different methods to answer this question. Some use **1. (powerful / entire)** radio telescopes. They hope to receive **2. (tools / messages)** from intelligent life on distant planets. Other scientists only **3. (search for / allow)** life in our solar system. But these scientists aren't only looking for intelligent life. They want to **4. (circle / identify)** any possible life forms. To do this, they have to test whether conditions on a planet would **5. (allow / contact)** any kind of life to exist.

B. Words in Context. Complete each sentence with the correct answer.

1. We measure **distance** in _____.
   a. kilometers (km) b. kilograms (kg)

2. Some examples of **tools** are _____.
   a. monkeys and dolphins   b. telephones and laptops

3. If you **contact** someone, you _____ him or her.
   a. meet or communicate with   b. research and write about

4. If you have lived in a place your **entire** life, you have lived there _____ of your life.
   a. some   b. all

5. If a spaceship **circles** a planet, it _____ the planet.
   a. goes around   b. lands on

Word Partnership Use *message* with verbs and adjectives:
(*v.*) **give** someone a message, **leave** a message, **take** a message, **get** a message, **send** a message; (*adj.*) **clear** message, **important** message, **powerful** message, **strong** message.

Satellite dishes in New Mexico, U.S.A.

Before You Read

A. Completion. Read the definitions. Complete the paragraph with the correct form of the words in **bold**.

astronaut: a person who travels into space

colony: a place or an area under the control of another place, usually another country

establish: to make or start something, such as a system or an organization

rocket: a vehicle used to travel to space

Robert Zubrin is a(n) **1.** _____ scientist; he designs spaceships. He thinks we should send **2.** _____ into space, but not just to visit. Zubrin wants to **3.** _____ a human **4.** _____ on the planet Mars. He wants to change the planet into a new place for humans to live.

B. Predict. Read the sentence below. Circle your answer and discuss your reasons with a partner. Then compare your ideas with those in the passage.

Sending humans into space to live (**is / is not**) a good idea because . . .

∧ This is how a Mars One colony might look like in the future.

LIVING IN SPACE

1　Stephen Hawking, one of the world's most important scientists, believes that to **survive**, humans must move into space: "Once we **spread out** into space and establish **independent** colonies, our future should be safe," he says.

5　Today, the European Union, India, China, Russia, and Japan are all planning to send astronauts back to Earth's closest **neighbor**: the moon. Some of these countries want to create space stations there between 2020 and 2030. These stations will prepare humans to visit and later live on Mars or other
10　Earthlike planets.

Robert Zubrin, a rocket scientist, thinks humans should colonize space. He wants to start with Mars. Why? He thinks sending people to Mars will allow us to learn a lot—for example, about the ability of humans to live in a very different
15　environment. Then we can eventually create new human societies on other planets. In addition, any **advances** we make in the fields of science, technology, **medicine**, and health will also **benefit** us here on Earth.

SpaceX is a company that builds rockets. Its owner, Elon Musk,
20　also believes we should colonize Mars, but he doesn't want just one small colony. He doesn't want to send just "one little **mission**;" he would like to send millions of people.

Not everyone thinks sending humans into space is a smart idea. Many say it's too expensive, even if it's just a short
25　**journey**. And most space trips are not short. A one-way trip to Mars, for example, would take about six months. People traveling this kind of distance face many health problems. Also, these first people would find life extremely difficult out in space. On the moon's **surface**, for example, the sun's rays[1] are
30　very dangerous. People would have to stay indoors most of the time.

Despite these concerns, sending people into space seems certain. In the future, we might see lunar[2] cities or even new human cultures on other planets. First stop: the moon.

⌃ Neil Armstrong, the first astronaut to walk on the surface of the moon

---

1　The **sun's rays** are narrow beams of light from the sun.
2　**Lunar** means "related to the moon."

Reading Comprehension

Multiple Choice. Choose the best answer for each question.

Purpose

1. What is the main purpose of this passage?
   a. to give reasons for and against space colonization
   b. to describe what life would be like on the moon
   c. to explain the history of human space travel
   d. to compare the environments of Mars and the moon

Reference

2. What does *our* in Stephen Hawking's quote *our future should be safe* (line 4) refer to?
   a. colonies'
   b. scientists'
   c. humans'
   d. astronauts'

Detail

3. Between 2020 and 2030, some countries plan to send astronauts to _____.
   a. Mars
   b. other Earthlike planets
   c. the moon
   d. another solar system

Detail

4. Why are some countries planning to create lunar space stations?
   a. to find out about the moon's surface
   b. to lower Earth's population
   c. to grow food for humans on Earth
   d. to prepare humans to live on other planets

Detail

5. Which reason for living in space is NOT mentioned?
   a. We can learn if humans can live in a very different environment.
   b. We can create human societies on other planets.
   c. We can search for life on other planets.
   d. We can benefit from scientific advances.

Main Idea

6. Which of the following is the main idea of the fifth paragraph?
   a. There are reasons not to send humans to space.
   b. Travel to space is very expensive.
   c. The sun's rays are dangerous for humans.
   d. People living on the moon will need to stay indoors.

Paraphrase

7. What does *First stop: the moon* mean in the last line?
   a. Everybody wants to go to the moon first.
   b. Mars's moon is the best place to have a human colony.
   c. All spaceships to other planets will stop at the moon first.
   d. The first human colony in space will likely be on the moon.

Did You Know?

The meals astronauts eat in space include food such as pasta and chocolate cake or, for Japanese astronauts, ramen noodles.

Reading Skill

Identifying Reasons (2)

A reading text will sometimes contain arguments for and against an idea. It can be useful to identify and list all the reasons for and against an idea. This can help you form your own opinion on a particular topic.

A. Analyzing. Look back at the reading on page 57. Read the third paragraph and identify the main idea of the paragraph. Then underline the reasons that support the main idea.

B. Completion. Now read the fifth paragraph of the reading on page 57. Complete the diagram below by writing the reasons in the boxes.

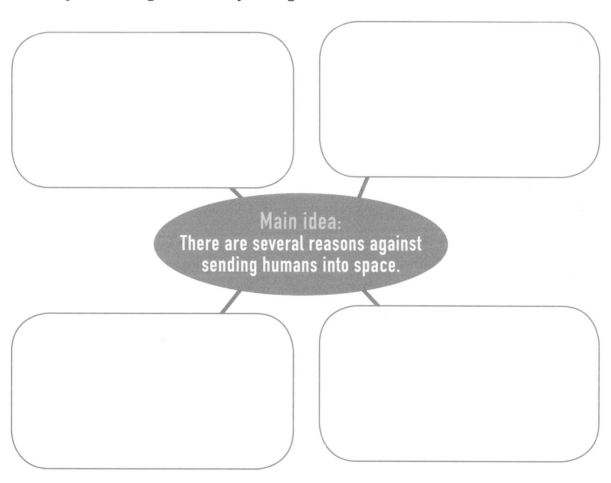

Main idea:
There are several reasons against sending humans into space.

Critical Thinking Discuss with a partner. Do you agree with Elon Musk that we should send millions of people to Mars? Why or why not? What do you think would be the most difficult thing about living in a colony in space?

Vocabulary Practice

A. Matching. Read the information and match each word in **red** with its definition.

A **mission** to Mars would take at least a year—six months to get there and six months to return. This sounds like a long time, but think about it—people from Europe used to go on six-month **journeys** to Australia by ship. What's more difficult than getting to Mars is living there. People who want to live on Mars will have to find water. They would need water to **survive**, and they would probably have to take it with them from Earth. But scientists think water existed on Mars in the past and may still be under the **surface** of the planet. So, in time, the planet might be able to have water again. This would then make people on Mars more **independent** from Earth.

1. _____: able to live on one's own

2. _____: the outer part of something

3. _____: a special trip that has an aim or a goal

4. _____: trips, travels

5. _____: to stay alive

B. Words in Context. Complete each sentence with the correct answer.

1. A **neighbor** is a person who lives _____ you.
   a. near   b. far from

2. A student of **medicine** probably wants to be a(n) _____.
   a. doctor   b. astronaut

3. If a group of people **spreads out**, they _____.
   a. come together in one place
   b. move away from one another

4. If we make **advances** in science or technology, we _____ in those areas.
   a. do worse   b. improve

5. If something **benefits** you, it _____ you.
   a. helps   b. hurts

> **Word Link** *in, im* = not: *in*dependent, *im*polite, *im*possible

⌄ A view of the water-ice clouds drifting over the ancient volcanoes on Mars

VIEWING Women in Space

Before You Watch

Discussion. Read about the U.S. space shuttle program. Then discuss the questions below.

The United States' space shuttle program, which began in 1981, sent shuttles to space 135 times. This program was important because it built shuttles that allowed smooth landing and could make multiple journeys to space and back. They also allowed up to eight astronauts to travel at a time. Shuttle missions brought supplies to the International Space Station, repaired satellites, and performed experiments in space. The last space shuttle mission was in 2011.

1. What are the advantages of a shuttle over other spacecraft?

2. Why do you think the program ended?

3. Who is Sally Ride? Why do you think she is famous?

Space Shuttle ❯ *Endeavour* launches into space.

❮ Astronaut Sally Ride was an American physicist who was a crew member on space shuttle *Challenger*, launched in 1983.

While You Watch

A. Matching. Look at these events. Match them (a–g) to the years on the timeline below.

a. Eileen Collins goes into space for the first time.

b. The space shuttle program begins.

c. Sally Ride goes into space for the first time.

d. Mae Jemison goes into space.

e. NASA begins.

f. Valentina Tereshkova goes into space.

g. The first man lands on the moon.

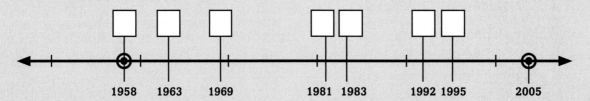

1958 1963 1969 1981 1983 1992 1995 2005

B. Matching. Match the information to the correct person.

a. was the first woman in space

b. was in space for six days

c. was the first African American woman in space

d. was the first American woman in space

e. was the first female shuttle pilot

f. flew into space in 1985, 1999, and 2005

g. was a doctor of medicine

h. was in space for three days

| **Eileen Collins** | ☐ ☐ | **Mae Jemison** | ☐ ☐ |
| **Sally Ride** | ☐ ☐ | **Valentina Tereshkova** | ☐ ☐ |

After You Watch

Discussion. Look at these other famous "space firsts." Then discuss the questions below with a partner.

1957 first animal in space (Laika the dog)

1959 first man-made object to land on moon (Lunar 2 probe)

1961 first person in space (Yuri Gagarin)

1965 first spacewalk (Alexei Leonov)

1976 first man-made object on Mars (Viking probes I and II)

1992 first married couple in space (Mark Lee and Jan Davis)

2013 first music video filmed in space (Chris Hadfield's *Space Oddity*)

1. Which of these "firsts" do you think was the greatest achievement? Why?

2. What other "space firsts" do you think will happen in the next 50 years? 100 years?

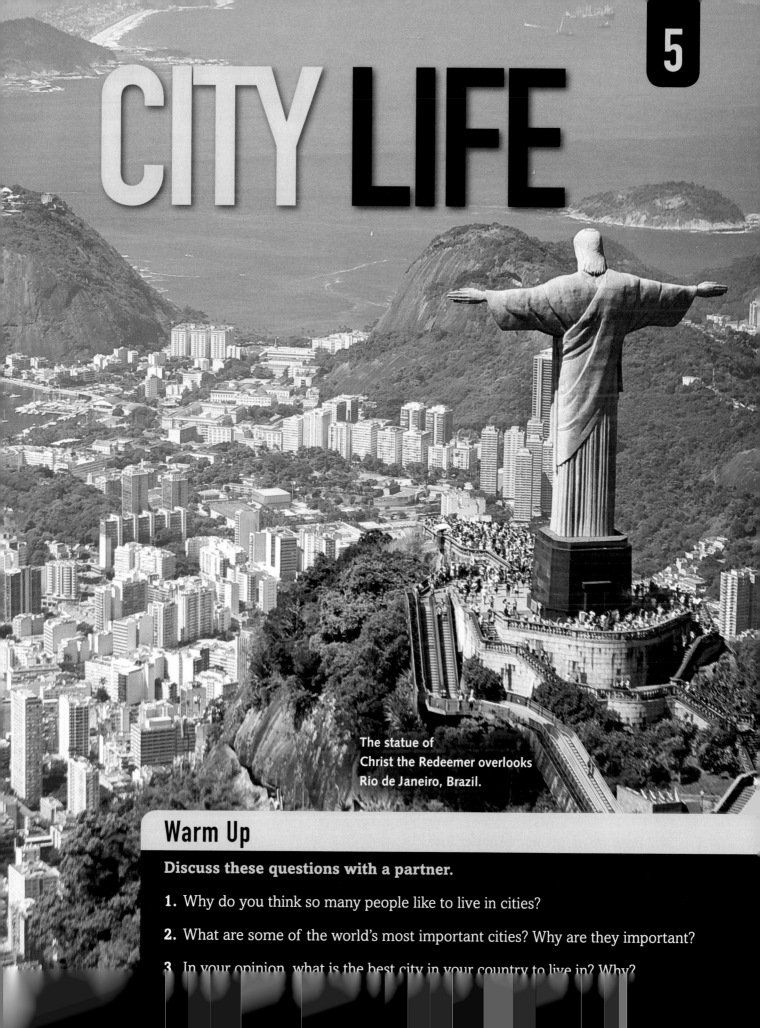

CITY LIFE

5

The statue of
Christ the Redeemer overlooks
Rio de Janeiro, Brazil.

Warm Up

Discuss these questions with a partner.

1. Why do you think so many people like to live in cities?

2. What are some of the world's most important cities? Why are they important?

3. In your opinion, what is the best city in your country to live in? Why?

GLOBAL CITIES

- 💲 Business
- 👥 People
- 📰 Media
- 🎭 Entertainment
- 🏛 Politics

15 Beijing CHINA
14 Toronto CANADA
13 Washington, D.C. U.S.
12 San Francisco U.S.
11 Brussels BELGIUM
10 Seoul SOUTH KOREA
9 Sydney AUSTRALIA
8 Singapore
7 Los Angeles U.S.

Before You Read

> The Global Cities Index is a list of the world's most powerful and important cities. There are 66 cities in total. The top 15 cities in 2011 are listed above. Each city gets a score in five areas.

A. Discussion. Study the chart above and read the information about the Global Cities Index. Then answer these questions.

1. Why do you think the city names are in different colors?

2. In what ways are the top four cities similar to and different from one another?

3. What do you think makes the top cities special?

B. Predict. Which city or cities do you think will become more important in the future? Complete the sentence and read the passage to check your ideas.

In the future, I think _____

will become more important because _____

_____

_____

_____.

6 Chicago U.S.

5 Hong Kong CHINA

4 Paris FRANCE

3 Tokyo JAPAN

2 London U.K.

1 New York City U.S.

John Tomanio and Lawson Parker, NGM Staff. Source: A. T. Kearney

The Global Cities Index

"New York City is a star—the city of cities," wrote author John Gunther. But why is New York—or London, Paris, or Tokyo—a great city? To answer this question, the creators of the Global Cities Index looked at five **factors**: business, people, media, entertainment, and politics.

Factor	What It Measures
Business	How many global companies are in the city? Does the city do a lot of **international** business?
People	Does the city **attract** talented[1] people from around the world? Are the city's universities good? How many residents have college degrees?
Media	Is it easy to get news and information from different **sources** (TV, radio, Internet)? How many residents have Internet **access**?
Entertainment	Does the city have many entertainment **options**: museums, sports, music, and different types of restaurants?
Politics	How many embassies[2] and international organizations[3] are in the city?

1 A **talented** person has special skills and can do something well.
2 An **embassy** is a government building where officials from a foreign country work.
3 An **organization** is a group of people. The members of an organization work together for a certain reason.

Future Leaders

As the chart on pages 64–65 shows, most cities on the Global Cities Index are strong in certain areas. Seoul's strength, for example, is business (it gets over five money icons), while Los Angeles's strength is people. New York, London, Paris, and Tokyo are at the top because they are strong in all five areas.

Which cities will be more powerful in the future? Creators of the Global Cities Index **predict** the most growth in the following areas:

- **Asia:** In China, cities such as Beijing and Shanghai will grow, **especially** in the area of business. In ten years, they may be as powerful as New York or Tokyo. Indian cities such as Mumbai and New Delhi also have a lot of business **potential**.

- **South America:** Rio de Janeiro and São Paulo in Brazil, and Bogotá in Colombia, will be more powerful. In these cities, the middle class[4] is growing, and life for many is improving.

- **The Middle East:** Istanbul and Ankara in Turkey, and Cairo in Egypt, will have more **influence** in international business and politics—especially in helping East and West work together.

In ten years, the top four cities on the index may be different, but one thing is certain. With over 50 percent of the world's population now living in urban areas, tomorrow's global cities will be more powerful than ever.

A dusk view of central Cairo

---

4 The **middle class** is a category of people. They earn more than the working class but less than the upper class. It includes professionals and business people.

Reading Comprehension

Multiple Choice. Choose the best answer for each question.

Gist

1. What is the reading mainly about?
   a. why certain global cities are important
   b. the fastest growing cities in the world
   c. global cities that are equally strong in many areas
   d. Asian cities that will be important in ten years

Purpose

2. What is the purpose of the chart at the bottom of page 65?
   a. to show the factors used to rank the cities
   b. to examine the reasons some cities scored poorly
   c. to show questions the researchers asked city leaders
   d. to describe why business is more important than politics

Detail

3. What is NOT covered in the Global Cities Index?
   a. food
   b. weather
   c. education
   d. sports

Detail

4. Which parts of the world are predicted to grow in the area of business?
   a. Asia and North America
   b. Asia and South America
   c. South America and the Middle East
   d. Asia and the Middle East

Reference

5. What does *many* refer to in line 20?
   a. many cities
   b. many people
   c. many businesses
   d. many times

Vocabulary

6. In line 26, what does *urban* refer to?
   a. cities and towns
   b. the future
   c. the globe
   d. political power

Did You Know?

It's believed that people in New York City speak over 800 different languages—the largest number of languages spoken in any city.

Inference

7. Which statement would the writer probably agree with?
   a. A global city is a powerful city.
   b. Fewer people will live in cities in the future.
   c. The global index will probably have the same cities ten years from now.
   d. Tomorrow's global cities will probably be less powerful than today's.

Understanding Charts and Graphs

Writers sometimes use charts and graphs to show information in a visual way. They can contain important details not mentioned in the text. One of the most common types of graphs is the bar graph. A bar graph uses either horizontal bars going across (also known as the *x*-axis) or vertical bars going up (also known as the *y* axis) to show comparisons among categories. One axis (either *x* or *y*) shows the specific categories being compared, and the other axis represents a certain value. For example:

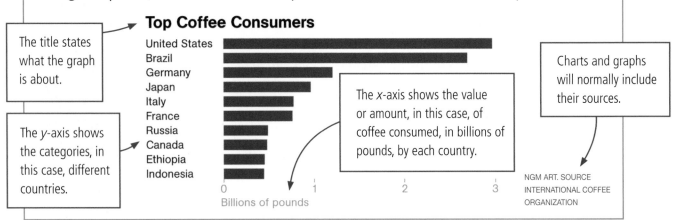

The title states what the graph is about.

The *y*-axis shows the categories, in this case, different countries.

Top Coffee Consumers

The *x*-axis shows the value or amount, in this case, of coffee consumed, in billions of pounds, by each country.

Charts and graphs will normally include their sources.

NGM ART. SOURCE
INTERNATIONAL COFFEE
ORGANIZATION

A. Understanding Charts and Graphs. Look back at the chart on pages 64–65. Then complete the description below.

The chart compares the world's most important and powerful
1. _____. Each city gets a score in **2.** _____
different areas as shown by the icons (small pictures). The purple icon is politics.
The orange one is **3.** _____. The **4.** _____
one is media. The blue one is **5.** _____, and the
6. _____ one is business.

B. Multiple Choice. Use the chart on pages 64–65 to answer each question.

1. Which city scores the highest for business?
   a. New York City   b. London   c. Paris   d. Tokyo

2. In what area does London score the highest?
   a. business   b. people   c. media   d. entertainment

3. How many cities have higher scores in politics than in entertainment?
   a. none   b. one   c. two   d. three

Critical Thinking Discuss with a partner. Which city in the chart on pages 64–65 would you like to live in the most? Why?

Vocabulary Practice

A. Matching. Read the information below. Then match each word in **red** with its definition.

Times Square in New York City **attracts** about 40 million people every year, including many **international** tourists. **Factors** that make Times Square such a popular place include a huge variety of entertainment **options**, such as movie theaters, restaurants, and shopping. It is **especially** famous for its Broadway shows.

1. _____: choices
2. _____: in particular
3. _____: involving two or more countries
4. _____: things that influence a result
5. _____: pulls; draws in

Times Square, in New York, is one of the world's most popular tourist attractions.

B. Words in Context. Complete each sentence with the correct answer.

1. If you have **access** to something, you have _____.

   a. a list of reasons to support it   b. a way to get or use it

2. A person who has **influence** over something has _____ it.

   a. power to change   b. questions about

3. When you **predict** something, you say something _____.

   a. never happened   b. will or might happen

4. If someone has **potential**, he or she has an ability that _____.

   a. cannot be developed   b. can be developed

5. Examples of **sources** of information might be _____.

   a. questions and ideas   b. newspapers and websites

> **Word Link** We can add **inter-** to some words to refer to things that move or happen between two or more things or people. (*She is taking an **inter**national flight.*) Other examples include ***inter**view*, ***inter**act*, and ***Inter**net*.

Before You Read

A. Discussion. Look at the photo and read the caption. Then answer the questions.

1. What is a *favela*? About how many people live in Rio's favelas?

2. Where are many of the favelas found?

3. What do you think life is like in a favela?

B. Predict. Read the title and the first paragraph of the reading on the next page. What is the reading mainly about? Circle your answer. Then read the passage to check your idea.

a. improvements in Rio's poorest neighborhoods

b. the history of Rio's neighborhoods

Rio de Janeiro is a major city in Brazil, with a population of over six million people. Almost a quarter of its people live in poor neighborhoods called *favelas*, such as this one on a Rio mountainside.

RIO REBORN

Rio de Janeiro

1　Around the world, Rio de Janeiro is famous for its beautiful beaches and Carnival celebration. But the city is also known for its poor areas, known as *favelas*. For years, many favelas had high poverty[1] and **crime** rates. However, things are starting to change.

5　In the past, many favelas **received** very little government assistance. Neighborhood **residents** had to build their own streets and homes. Gangs[2] were also **common**, and so were guns. However, a new government plan is starting to change this. The city is sending thousands of police officers into favelas with the goal of driving out[3] 10　the gangs. In some favelas, the plan is already working. Crime is down, and unlike in the past, children are playing in the streets again. New apartment buildings are being built, and the city is **providing** more services. "In 20 years," says police officer Leonardo Nogueira, "the children who live here now . . . will be different people."

15　Police influence is changing the favelas, but something else is, too. Today, more Brazilians are **moving into** these neighborhoods because housing is expensive in other parts of Rio. "Favelas are a place for young doctors without much money to get started and young architects to start working," explains Simone Miranda, a Rio tour 20　guide. In the past, favela residents felt different—**separate** from the rest of Rio. "But now," says Miranda, "they feel part of the society of Brazil."

Life is improving in the favelas, but there are still challenges. In some areas, poverty rates are still high. As students, families, and foreigners 25　move into the favelas, **property** costs skyrocket. In some places, housing has more than doubled in price. Despite this, favela residents are hopeful. If Rio can **develop** these favelas for *all* residents—both poor and middle class—the city could become a **model** for other cities with similar problems.

---

1 **Poverty** is the state of being very poor.
2 A **gang** is a group of (usually young) people. They go around together and often make trouble.
3 To **drive out** is to chase away.

Reading Comprehension

Multiple Choice. Choose the best answer for each question.

Gist

1. Another title for this reading could be _____.
   a. A History of Rio's Favelas
   b. Crime on the Rise in Rio's Favelas
   c. Favelas, Rio's New Tourist Destination
   d. How Rio's Favelas Are Changing

Detail

2. Which of these things found in favelas is NOT mentioned in the reading?
   a. art
   b. guns
   c. gangs
   d. poverty

Detail

3. What was true about favelas in the past?
   a. They got a lot of government assistance.
   b. There were no gangs.
   c. Many police officers worked there.
   d. Children didn't play in the streets very much.

Inference

4. Which statement would tour guide Simone Miranda probably agree with?
   a. More favela residents now feel a part of Brazilian culture.
   b. The police officers in the favelas cause many problems.
   c. Young people from Rio should not move into the favelas.
   d. There will be no more favelas in 20 years.

Purpose

5. What is the purpose of the third paragraph?
   a. to discuss the high costs of housing in Rio
   b. to explain why architects are choosing to study in favelas
   c. to talk about how newer residents are changing the favelas
   d. to compare favela and non-favela residents

Vocabulary

6. In line 25, what does *skyrocket* mean?
   a. to increase quickly
   b. to drop slowly
   c. to become dangerous
   d. to become smaller

Reference

7. What can you replace *this* with in the following sentence:
   Despite this, favela residents are hopeful (lines 26–27).
   a. these areas
   b. these foreigners
   c. these cheap houses
   d. these challenges

Did You Know?

In 1996, Michael Jackson filmed a part of the video for *They Don't Really Care About Us* at the Santa Marta favela.

Understanding a Writer's Use of Quotes

A writer may choose to include the exact words from a source. These are set off by quotation marks (" "). Quoting can be done for various reasons, such as the following:

To add a supporting statement or question:

Locals aren't waiting for others to solve their problems. "It's important for us to fix things ourselves," said one favela resident.

To provide expert evidence for an argument:

Both countries need closer ties. "I consider the relationship with the U.S. very important to Brazil," said Brazil president Dilma Rousseff.

To highlight an interesting or memorable phrase:

Many tourists visit favelas, but some people feel this "poverty tourism" is not appropriate.

A. Scanning. Look back at the reading on page 71 again. Underline the quotes. Discuss with a partner: Why did the writer include them?

B. Identifying Purpose. What do you think is the purpose for the following quotes?

1. Rio has many problems including poverty, crime, and low wages. "It happens in the whole world, but I would say here the [problems are] greater," says José Mariano Beltrame, State Secretary of Public Security.

   a. to provide expert evidence for an argument

   b. to highlight a memorable phrase

2. The area around the Olympic stadium is full of cars and malls but little else that makes it special. The place is known as "the Rio that forgot it is Rio."

   a. to provide expert evidence for an argument

   b. to highlight an interesting or memorable phrase

3. Favela resident Sérgio Souza de Andrade explains that people fear the future without the police. "What will happen when they leave?" he asks.

   a. to add a supporting statement or question

   b. to highlight an interesting or memorable phrase

Critical Thinking Discuss with a partner. Do you think it is a good thing that more people from other parts of society are moving into the favelas? Give reasons for your answer.

A. Completion.

Complete the information by circling the correct word or phrase in each pair.

Favela Tours

If you visit Rio, should you visit a favela? Favela tours may be popular, but not everyone agrees they are a good idea.

At its best, a favela tour allows visitors to see a favela up close. Some tours also **1. (provide / move into)** jobs for **2. (residents / property)** (e.g., as guides, drivers, and artists). The local people earn money, which can then be used to help **3. (move into / develop)** the favela.

While some favelas **4. (receive / move into)** money from tours, sometimes little is actually given back to the neighborhood. In addition, some people feel that favelas are much like zoos, with visitors in buses kept **5. (separate / common)** from the people living there.

It's important, too, to remember that a favela can be dangerous. **6. (Crime / Model)** remains a problem, and a tour operator cannot ensure a visitor's safety.

B. Words in Context.

Complete each sentence with the correct answer.

1. If something acts as a **model** for something, it's a _____ example.
   a. good
   b. bad

2. When you **move into** a neighborhood, you _____.
   a. begin to live there
   b. leave it forever

3. If something is **common**, it _____.
   a. rarely happens
   b. happens often

4. A person who owns **property** owns _____.
   a. land
   b. animals

∧ Boys surrounded by colorful buildings in Santa Marta favela

> **Word Partnership** Use *separate* with nouns:
> separate **rooms**, separate **lives**, separate **beds**,
> separate **paths**.

VIEWING High-Rise Challenge

Before You Watch

A. Discussion. Read the information on one of New York City's newest high-rise buildings. Then discuss the questions below with a partner.

Name: One Bryant Park

Location: New York City

Year begun: 2004

Year completed: 2009

Height: 290 meters

Height including spire: 365 meters

Number of floors: 55

Earth removed for foundation: 198,000 cubic meters

Building cost: 1 billion dollars

1. How long did the building take to complete?

2. What part of the building do you think the spire is? How tall is it?

3. What part of the building do you think the foundation is?

4. What do you think was challenging about building One Bryant Park?

One Bryant Park, one of ❯ New York City's tallest skyscrapers, is located on Sixth Avenue, opposite Bryant Park.

While You Watch

A. Noticing. Check (✓) the challenges of building a high-rise that the video discusses.

☐ digging the foundation

☐ bringing materials to the building site

☐ working in bad weather

☐ lifting materials up to the building

☐ driving big trucks in city traffic

☐ putting things together high above the ground

☐ causing things to drop on the ground

B. Completion. Circle the correct word or phrase to complete each sentence.

One Bryant Park is on the corner of (**5th Avenue / 6th Avenue**).

The crane operator is so high he is not able to (**talk with others / see what he's lifting**).

The (**size / shape**) of the water tank makes it difficult to place.

The building's spire is put together (**on / above**) the ground.

After You Watch

Critical Thinking. Discuss these questions with a partner.

1. What are some advantages—and disadvantages—of living in a high-rise building like One Bryant Park?

2. One Bryant Park cost a billion dollars to complete. What do you think made it so expensive?

6

SMALL WORLDS

The yellow eggs of a
Large White butterfly
under a microscope

Warm Up

Discuss these questions with a partner.

1. What are some things that are too small to see with the human eye?

2. Have you ever looked at something under a microscope? What was it?

3. In what ways do you think very small creatures can be useful to us?

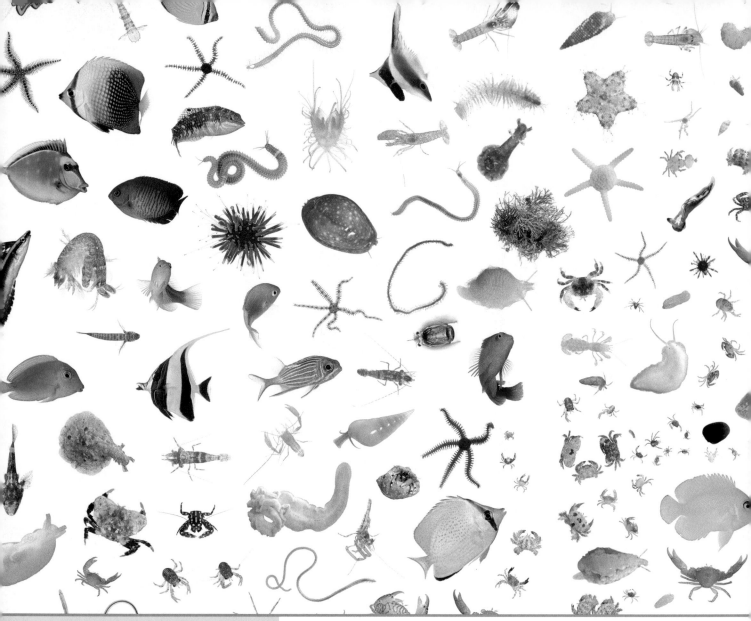

Around us there are millions of these **tiny** plants, insects, fish, and other animals, but we rarely see them. Most of these **organisms** live in the **soil**, or (like the ones pictured) in the water. Some are only a centimeter in size.

Before You Read

A. Matching. Look at the photo and read the caption. Match each word in **bold** with its definition.

1. very small in size _____

2. living things that can function on their own _____

3. dirt on the ground where plants grow _____

B. Predict. Read the first paragraph on page 79. What do you think E.O. Wilson means? In what ways are tiny creatures important? Tell a partner. Then read the passage to check your ideas.

IN ONE CUBIC FOOT

1　In any **environment**—forest, mountain, water—you always
　see the big animals first: birds, mammals, fish. But under
　your feet, on land or in the water, there are many smaller
　organisms: insects, tiny plants, miniature sea creatures.[1] They
5　seem unimportant, but, in fact, these sea creatures and ground
　dwellers[2] are "the heart of life on Earth," says naturalist E.O.
　Wilson. Without them, our world would change **dramatically**.

The Cycle of Life

　Most organisms on Earth live on the ground or just below it.
10　Here, they are part of an important **cycle**. Plants and animals
　fall to the ground when they die. Later, tiny insects and other
　organisms break down[3] the dead plant and animal material. This
　process eventually returns nutrients[4] to the soil and gives plants
　energy. Plants can then help to **maintain** a healthy environment
15　for humans and other animals.

1　A **creature** is an animal of
　some kind.

2　A **dweller** is a person or
　thing that lives in a certain
　place.

3　If you **break** something
　down, you break it into
　smaller pieces.

4　**Nutrients** are substances
　(like vitamins) that help
　plants and animals grow.

Discoveries in a Cube

Despite their importance, scientists know very little about most ground organisms. To learn more, photographer
20 David Liittschwager went to different places around the world, including a forest, a river, a mountain, and a coral reef. In each place, he put a green 12-inch (30 cm) cube on the ground or in the water. Then he and his **team** counted and photographed the organisms that lived in
25 or moved through the cube. Often they **discovered** hundreds, some only a millimeter in size. "It was like finding little gems,"[5] he says.

---

5 **Gems** are beautiful stones used in jewelry.

⌄ Coral Reef

Moorea, French Polynesia

Here, Liittschwager saw thousands of creatures in the cube and photographed over 600. The team identified as many as possible, but it was difficult. Many of the animals they found were new species.

baby octopus
1.1 cm (0.45 in) across

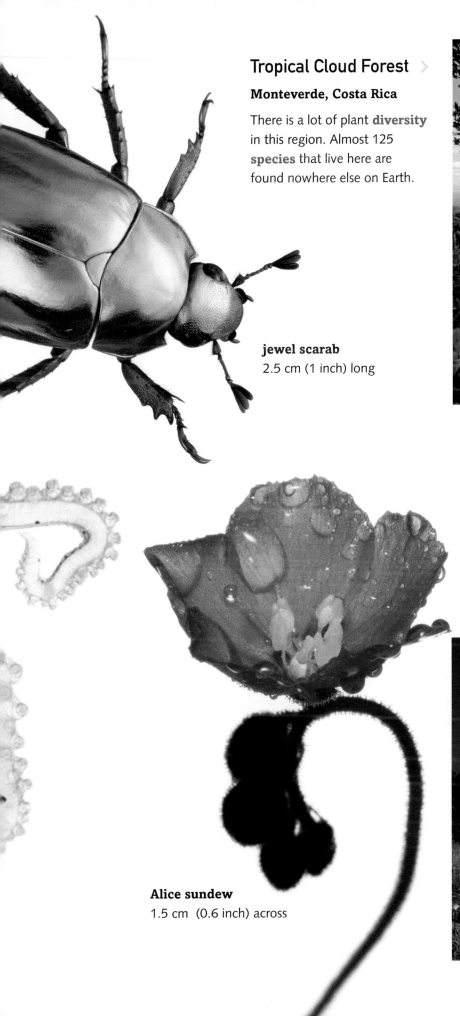

Tropical Cloud Forest >

Monteverde, Costa Rica

There is a lot of plant **diversity** in this region. Almost 125 **species** that live here are found nowhere else on Earth.

jewel scarab
2.5 cm (1 inch) long

∨ Mountain Fynbos

Table Mountain, South Africa

Large animals live here, but most creatures in this region are very small. Inside the cube, Liittschwager's team identified some of these: over 90 separate species found, 25 being plants just on the soil surface.

Alice sundew
1.5 cm (0.6 inch) across

Reading Comprehension

Multiple Choice. Choose the best answer for each question.

Gist

1. Another title for this reading could be _____.
a. Dangers to Ground Creatures
b. The Importance of Tiny Organisms
c. Saving Small Animals in Cubes
d. The Life of Nutrients

Vocabulary

2. In line 4, *miniature* means _____.
a. very small
b. very large
c. very beautiful
d. very important

Detail

3. Where do most organisms on Earth live?
a. in the sea
b. on or just below the ground
c. deep underground
d. in the air

Main Idea

4. Liittschwager and his team used the cube to _____.
a. collect different species for research
b. count and photograph animal species
c. test the quality of the soil and water
d. protect animals from human activities

Reference

5. In line 17, *their* refers to _____.
a. scientists
b. ground organisms
c. cubes
d. nutrients

Detail

6. Why was it difficult to identify the creatures at the coral reef?
a. Many were new to science.
b. The water was cloudy.
c. They were too small.
d. Many of them looked the same.

Inference

7. Why does Liittschwager call the organisms *little gems* in line 27?
a. They are difficult for him to see.
b. He thinks they are valuable and precious.
c. Many of the organisms are shiny.
d. The organisms look like little stones.

Did You Know?

Many thousands of species—mostly different types of bacteria—live in a single gram of garden soil. Most are still unknown to science.

Understanding Sequence

When you sequence events, you put them in the order in which they occur. Sequencing is important for gaining a deeper understanding of the relationship between events in a process. Some common words that can signal sequence are *after*, *then*, *later*, *once*, *when*, and *as soon as*. One way to show sequence is to list the events in a chain diagram.

> ∨ David Liittschwager discovered and photographed hundreds of species living in this 3,200-year-old giant sequoia tree called The President.

A. Analyzing. Read the second paragraph of the reading passage again. Underline signal words or phrases that indicate a sequence.

B. Sequencing. Put the life cycle events (a–f) in order in the diagram.

   a. Plants and animals die.
   b. Living plants get energy from the nutrients in the soil.
   c. Plants help to support life for animals and humans.
   d. Dead material is broken down.
   e. Dead plants and animals fall to the ground.
   f. Nutrients are returned to the soil.

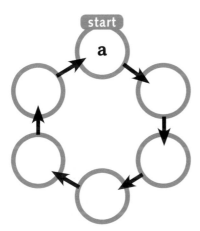

Critical Thinking Discuss with a partner. Where in your area would you look for tiny organisms? What do you think you might find? In what ways do you think the world would change if there were no tiny creatures?

Vocabulary Practice

A. Completion. Complete the passage by circling the correct word in each word pair.

One of the smallest animals in the world is a type of insect called a fairyfly. The male fairyfly of one **1. (species / cycle)** is only 0.17 millimeters in length—about the size of the period at the end of this sentence. Not much is known about the life **2. (cycle / energy)** of fairyflies. But we do know they don't live long—between only 2 and 11 days.

Fairyflies can live in many different **3. (processes / environments)**. For example, they can stay underwater for up to 15 days. However, most of them are found in rain forests. The areas with the greatest fairyfly **4. (energy / diversity)** are in Australia, New Zealand, and South America.

While fairyflies are considered to be one of the world's smallest animals, one day scientists may **5. (discover / maintain)** even smaller creatures.

B. Words in Context. Complete each sentence with the correct answer.

1. A **process** is a series of actions that _____ something.

   a. stops   b. produces

2. A **dramatic** event is _____.

   a. big and sudden   b. small and quiet

3. If you **maintain** a healthy weight, it _____.

   a. changes often   b. doesn't change much

4. Humans receive **energy** from _____.

   a. soil   b. food

5. A **team** is a group of people who _____.

   a. work together   b. live together

∧ The fairyfly is one of the world's smallest animals.

Word Partnership

Use **environment** with: (*v.*) **protect the** environment, **save the** environment, **maintain the** environment; (*adj.*) **natural** environment, **healthy** environment, **physical** environment.

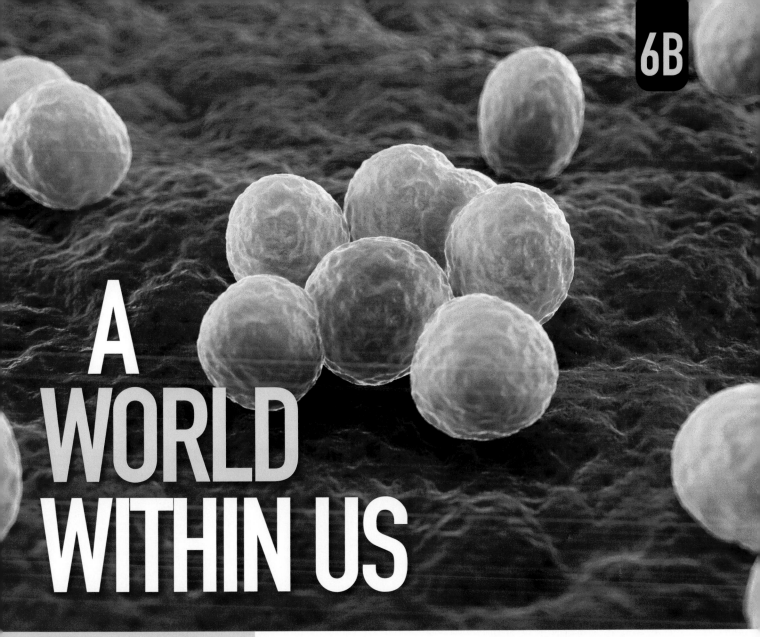

A WORLD WITHIN US

Before You Read

A. True or False? Look at the photo and read the caption. What do you know about bacteria? Circle **T** (True) or **F** (False).

1. You have more bacteria in your body than human cells.   **T**   **F**

2. In our body, most bacteria is in our mouth.   **T**   **F**

3. Most bacteria in our bodies are dangerous to us.   **T**   **F**

4. Antibiotics[2] can be bad for us.   **T**   **F**

B. Skimming. Read the passage on pages 86–87. Check your answers in **A**.

∧ Bacteria are microscopic[1] organisms. Some like Staphylococcus aureus can cause harm.

---

1 If something is **microscopic**, it is very small. You can only see it with a microscope.

2 **Antibiotics** are a type of medicine that stops bacterial infections.

1 | Life in Miniature

Bacteria: They're **invisible**. They're everywhere. And we need them to live.

In our bodies, bacteria outnumber human cells by ten
5 to one. All this bacteria weighs as much as your brain—nearly three pounds (1.3 kilograms). Most bacteria in our bodies are not **harmful**; in fact, many benefit us in important ways. They help us digest[1] food. They make important vitamins, and they help fight **infections**.

10 But some bacteria can be dangerous. Take, for example, *Staphylococcus aureus*. It lives in our noses. Usually, it's **harmless**; other bacteria in the nose control it. But if *S. aureus* travels to another environment, things change. In the skin, for example, it can cause **deadly** infections.

---

1 When you **digest** food, your stomach uses the food it needs and removes the rest.

1 IN 10 CELLS
in the body is human.

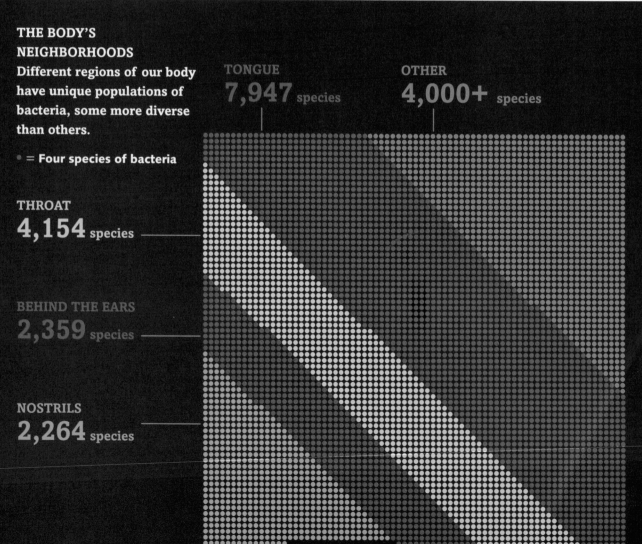

THE BODY'S NEIGHBORHOODS
Different regions of our body have unique populations of bacteria, some more diverse than others.

● = Four species of bacteria

THROAT
4,154 species

BEHIND THE EARS
2,359 species

NOSTRILS
2,264 species

TONGUE
7,947 species

OTHER
4,000+ species

15 We **cure** most bacterial infections with antibiotics, but there are problems with this medicine. Antibiotics kill bad, infection-causing bacteria. But this medicine kills good bacteria in our bodies, too. When we kill the good kind, this can cause other health problems. A **lack of** certain bacteria in the body can make us sick.

20 So what can we do? We should not use antibiotics very often, say scientists. We can fight infections, but we also need to maintain helpful bacteria in the body. To help us do this, doctors are now developing "probiotic remedies." These new medicines will return certain bacteria to the body and **restore** the **balance** our
25 body needs.

For years, we thought all bacteria were dangerous. Of course, some are. But we are learning that many bacteria keep us healthy. They live on and within us, and our well-being **depends on** them.

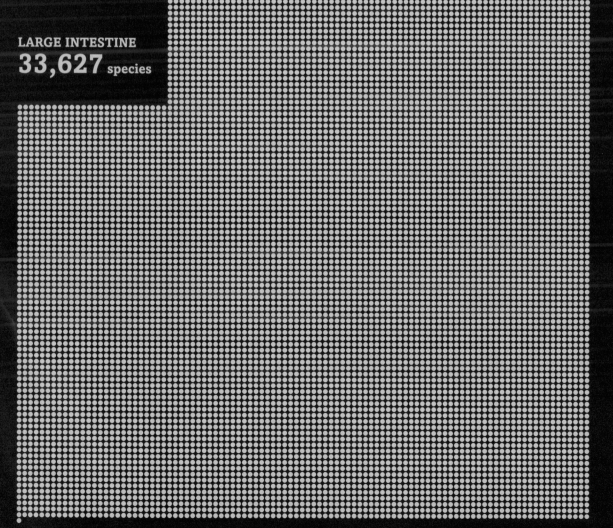

LARGE INTESTINE
33,627 species

Reading Comprehension

Multiple Choice. Choose the best answer for each question.

Purpose

1. What is the purpose of this reading?
   a. to describe how bacteria are important to our bodies
   b. to examine the dangers of bacterial infections
   c. to compare the bacteria that live inside and outside our body
   d. to explain why we should avoid antibiotics

Detail

2. Which statement about bacteria is true?
   a. The bacteria in our brain weigh three pounds.
   b. Most bacteria in our bodies are dangerous.
   c. We cannot live without bacteria.
   d. There are more bacteria in our nostrils than in our throat.

Paraphrase

3. In lines 4–5, it says *In our bodies, bacteria outnumber human cells by ten to one.* What does this mean?
   a. There are more bacteria than human cells.
   b. There are more human cells than bacteria.
   c. There are ten human cells for every bacteria cell.
   d. There are ten bacteria in every human cell.

Purpose

4. What is the purpose of the third paragraph?
   a. to describe why people get skin infections
   b. to warn us against *Staphylococcus aureus*
   c. to list the dangers of *Staphylococcus aureus*
   d. to explain why some bacteria can be dangerous

Reference

5. What does *it* in line 14 refer to?
   a. bacteria in the nose
   b. *Staphylococcus aureus*
   c. dangerous infections
   d. bacteria in the skin

Detail

6. What can "probiotic remedies" do?
   a. get healthy bacteria back in the body
   b. fight against some antibiotics
   c. identify good vs. bad bacteria
   d. increase good and bad bacteria in the body

Vocabulary

7. In line 28, what does *well-being* mean?
   a. medicine
   b. health
   c. body
   d. bacteria

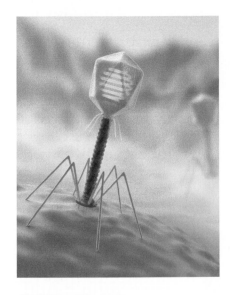

Did You Know?

Bacteria-infecting viruses known as phages are the most common form of life on Earth. There are more phages than stars in the universe. More than a trillion (1,000,000,000,000) exist in a human body.

Understanding Pros and Cons

Writers will often discuss both the pros (good points) and the cons (bad points) of a piece of information or an issue. Understanding both sides is a useful way to consider an issue. It can also help you decide your own opinion. When taking notes on a text that includes both pros and cons, it can be helpful to list them in two columns.

A. Determining Pros and Cons. Look at this information about bacteria in our body. Mark each one **P** (pro) or **C** (con).

1. _____: Bacteria help fight infections.

2. _____: Bacteria can cause infections.

3. _____: Bacteria help us to digest food.

4. _____: Bacteria make vitamins.

B. Identifying Pros and Cons. Read paragraph 4 on page 87 again. Then complete the chart below with the pros and cons of taking antibiotics.

Pros of taking antibiotics	Cons of taking antibiotics

⌃ Antibiotic medicine is a common way to treat illnesses, but it can cause problems, too.

Critical Thinking Discuss with a partner. Bad bacteria in food can lead to stomach infections. What foods do you think cause this? What can people do to avoid getting sick?

Vocabulary Practice

A. Matching. Read the information below. Then match each word in **red** with its definition.

Bacteria are organisms made up of just one cell. They live between other cells. Viruses, on the other hand, live inside cells. And while some bacteria can make us sick, most are **harmless**. All viruses, however, are **harmful**.

Viruses are 10 to 100 times smaller than bacteria, but both are **invisible** to humans. Unlike bacteria, viruses **depend on** living plants or animals to multiply and survive. Bacteria can live nearly anywhere, even on non-living surfaces.

Antibiotics cannot **cure** you of a viral **infection** such as the flu. They only kill bacteria. Many people have chicken soup, hot tea with lemon, or chili peppers to help them get better.

1. causing damage _____

2. not causing damage _____

3. impossible to see _____

4. help in healing _____

5. to need in order to survive _____

6. a disease or an illness _____

B. Words in Context. Complete each sentence with the correct answer.

1. You have **balance** when both sides of something are _____.

   a. heavy   b. equal

2. If you have a **lack of** support, you have _____.

   a. a lot of support   b. no support

3. To **restore** something means to _____.

   a. make it like it was   b. hide it from others

4. Something that is **deadly** can _____ you.

   a. kill   b. cure

Word Link

We can add the suffixes **-ful** (meaning "full of") and **-less** (meaning "without") to some nouns to form adjectives. Some nouns take *-ful* (e.g., *wonderful*), some take *-less* (e.g., *worthless*), and some can take both (e.g., *harmful / harmless*).

VIEWING Under Yellowstone

Before You Watch

A. Matching. Look at the photo and read the caption. Then match each word in **bold** with its definition.

∧ Steam rises from a **hot spring** in Yellowstone National Park, U.S.A. Scientists have recently discovered **strange** kinds of **microbes** living in this extremely hot **environment**. These tiny creatures are unlike any other type of life on the planet.

1. unusual, different from normal _____

2. very, very small life forms _____

3. surroundings in which a plant or an animal lives _____

4. a place where heated water flows from the ground _____

B. Discussion. Discuss these questions in a group.

1. What do you know about Yellowstone National Park?

2. Why do you think scientists are studying the microbes in the hot springs?

While You Watch

A. Noticing. Check (✓) the topics that are discussed.

☐ dangers from wolves and bears   ☐ creatures that survive in hot springs

☐ temperatures of hot springs   ☐ different types of microbes

☐ what microbes eat   ☐ possible life on other planets

B. Completion. Complete each sentence by circling the correct word in each pair.

The water in hot springs can reach temperatures of (**200 / 275**) degrees Celsius.

If you remove microbes from their hot springs environment, they (**grow / die**).

In the 1970s, scientists added a new branch to the tree of life called (**Bacteria / Archaea**).

Scientists hope to find (**gases / microbes**), similar to those in Yellowstone, on Mars or other planets.

After You Watch

Completion. Complete the summary with the words from the box. There is one extra word.

discovered	environment	explored	information	life	perfect	similar	universe

A group of scientists is studying the microbes in the hot springs at Yellowstone National Park. The very hot **1.** _____ of these hot springs is **2.** _____ for microbes.

In the 1970s, scientists **3.** _____ a new group of organisms in the hot springs, which they called Archaea. This group may give scientists **4.** _____ about what early life forms on Earth were like, and also show how **5.** _____ evolved.

Scientists think that these life forms may show whether life exists elsewhere in the **6.** _____. If there is indeed life beyond Earth, it may be very **7.** _____ to the microbes found in Yellowstone's hot springs.

7

WHEN DINOSAURS RULED

Children admire dinosaur skeletons at the Museum of Indianapolis, U.S.A.

Warm Up

Discuss these questions with a partner.

1. Do you know when dinosaurs lived?

2. Have you ever seen a movie about dinosaurs? Describe it.

3. Why do you think people are interested in dinosaurs?

Before You Read

Period	Years ago (millions)	
Triassic	248–206	Earth's warm and dry temperatures were perfect for **reptiles**. The oldest known dinosaur, discovered by **paleontologists** in Madagascar, dates to this time.
Jurassic	206–144	Some dinosaurs grew to huge sizes during this period.
Cretaceous	144–65	Dinosaurs became **extinct** at the end of this period.

A. Discussion. Look at the information and captions, paying attention to the words in **bold**. Then answer the questions below.

1. What kind of animals were dinosaurs? When did they die out?

2. What does a *paleontologist* do?

3. What does *extinct* mean?

B. Predict. Read the three question headings on page 96 and answer **Yes** or **No**. Then read the passage to check your answers.

With its long, sharp teeth, *Masiakasaurus* was a powerful predator.

When: 65–70 million years ago

Where: Madagascar

Tupuxuara, a type of flying dinosaur, had wings that measured 5.2 meters from tip to tip.

When: 115–112 million years ago

Where: Brazil

THE TRUTH ABOUT DINOSAURS

1   For years, scientists thought dinosaurs were big, cold-blooded, and not very smart—in other words, just **giant** reptiles. Some dinosaurs *were* huge. But many were about the size of modern-day birds or dogs. Were dinosaurs warm- or cold-blooded? Paleontologists are not
5   sure. But they believe a few were intelligent. Some smaller dinosaurs— like the two-meter (six-foot) *Troodon*—had **fairly** large brains.

Was *T. rex* a powerful predator?

While some scientists think *Tyrannosaurus rex* was a powerful predator, others think the opposite is true. For example, in the
10 movies, *T. rex* is often a fast-moving giant. **In reality**, this dinosaur could not run as fast. **Physically**, it was too large, so it probably moved about as fast as an elephant. *T. rex* also had very small arms and probably wasn't a powerful **hunter**. It may have been a scavenger
15 instead, eating dead animals.

Could dinosaurs fly?

Some reptiles, known as pterosaurs, were able to fly. But these were not dinosaurs, even though they looked like them.
20 Pterosaurs such as *Tupuxuara* could probably fly up to 16,000 kilometers (10,000 miles) nonstop. Scientists believe pterosaurs were actually very
25 **heavy**. So they probably could not take off[1] from the ground like birds. Instead, they first had to drop or throw themselves from trees
30 to fly, much like bats.

Are all dinosaurs extinct?

Dinosaurs **completely** disappeared about 65 million years ago.
35 Scientists believe they died out because of a global **climate** change: The Earth's temperature was too cold for them to survive. Now you can only see them in **museums**. However, they believe modern-day
40 birds are, in fact, dinosaurs' descendants. If this is true, then dinosaurs' **relatives** are still walking—and flying—among us!

Tyrannosaurus rex (T. rex)

---

1 If you **take off**, you leave the ground and start to fly.

Reading Comprehension

Multiple Choice. Choose the best answer for each question.

Gist

1. Another title for this reading could be _____.
   a. What Really Killed the Dinosaurs?
   b. Dinosaurs: Myths and Realities
   c. The Life of a Paleontologist
   d. Dinosaurs' New Relatives

Inference

2. Which statement about *Troodon* is probably true?
   a. It was the size of a dog.
   b. It was warm-blooded.
   c. It was a huge animal.
   d. It was quite intelligent.

Vocabulary

3. Some paleontologists think *T. rex* was a *scavenger* (line 14). What does this mean?
   a. It had small arms.
   b. It was a powerful killer.
   c. It was similar to an elephant.
   d. It ate dead animals.

Reference

4. In line 25, what does *they* refer to?
   a. pterosaurs
   b. scientists
   c. dinosaurs
   d. bats

Detail

5. What is true about *Tupuxuara*?
   a. They could fly very long distances.
   b. They were a type of bird.
   c. They looked very different from dinosaurs.
   d. They could take off from the ground.

Detail

6. What happened 65 million years ago?
   a. Some dinosaurs started to fly.
   b. Humans appeared on Earth.
   c. The last dinosaurs died out.
   d. Most birds became extinct.

Detail

7. Which sentence about dinosaurs is NOT true?
   a. Many kinds of dinosaurs could fly.
   b. Some dinosaurs had quite large brains.
   c. *T. rex* was too large to run very fast.
   d. Some scientists believe that birds are related to dinosaurs.

Did You Know?

Stegosaurus had a brain the size of a walnut, weighing just 75 grams.

Supporting Ideas with Examples

Writers often use examples to support their ideas. This is important when you make a claim (say that something is true), like in a persuasive essay. Supporting a claim with examples—or *evidence*—makes it more believable. Examples can also help explain difficult concepts.

Examples take different forms. Words that signal examples in a text include *for example, like,* and *such as*. Other examples may be in quotations, diagrams, and pictures.

A. Noticing. Circle the signaling words in these sentences and underline the examples.

1. Pterosaurs such as *Tupuxuara* could fly up to 16,000 kilometers (10,000 miles) nonstop.
2. Instead, they had to first drop or throw themselves from trees to fly, much like bats.
3. For example, in the movies, *T. rex* is often a fast-moving giant.

B. Completion. Complete each sentence with an example from the box (a–f). One example is extra.

a. *Brachiosaurus* weighed 80 tons	**b.** grass and leaves	**c.** *Stegosaurus*
d. *Jurassic Park* and *Godzilla*	**e.** sharp points on their tails	**f.** jellyfish

1. Some dinosaurs, like _____, had brains the size of a walnut.
2. To defend themselves from predators, some plant-eating dinosaurs had natural protection, such as _____.
3. Some animals have been on Earth longer than dinosaurs. For example, _____ have existed for 650 million years.
4. Many dinosaurs were heavy. For example, _____. That's 17 African elephants!
5. There have been many movies about dinosaurs, such as _____.

Critical Thinking Discuss with a partner. Why do you think many people have wrong ideas about dinosaurs? What other questions about dinosaurs would you want to find answers to?

Vocabulary Practice

A. Matching. Read the information and match each word in **red** with its definition.

For centuries, stories about **giant** sea monsters have existed in many countries. One of the most famous is Scotland's Loch Ness Monster (often called "Nessie"). **In reality**, some animals that were like Nessie lived in the world's seas 65–250 million years ago. For example, Nessie is **physically** similar to a type of plesiosaur—a sea reptile with a very long neck. But is Nessie really an ancient sea monster, still alive in a lake in Scotland? Probably not. Plesiosaurs (like the dinosaurs) died out **completely** about 65 million years ago.

1. actually, in fact _____
2. huge, very large _____
3. totally _____
4. related to the body _____

B. Completion. Complete the information by circling the correct word in each pair.

The ancient sea monster *Dakosaurus* is a **1. (museum / relative)** of modern-day crocodiles. This large and **2. (heavy / fairly)** South American sea reptile was a powerful **3. (climate / hunter)**. Sea reptiles like *Dakosaurus* were dangerous predators. Some, such as *Tylosaurus* (pictured), even ate sharks. But in the end, it was the sharks that survived. Today, you can only see *Dakosaurus* bones in a **4. (relative / museum)**, but sharks are found all over the world.

> **Word Link** We can add **-er** or **-or** to form nouns that describe a person who does a certain action or job, for example, *hunter* or *inventor*.

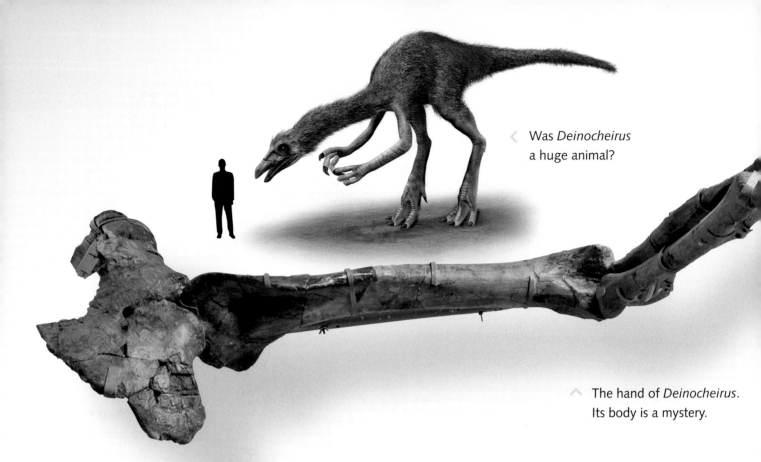

Was *Deinocheirus* a huge animal?

The hand of *Deinocheirus*. Its body is a mystery.

Before You Read

A. Completion. Read the definitions. Then complete the paragraph below with the correct form of the words in **bold**.

claws: the long, sharp nails on the toes or fingers of some animals
fossils: the bones or remains of an animal or a plant
horns: the hard things on top of an animal's head
unearth: to take something out of the ground

Paleontologists continue to **1.** _____ new dinosaur **2.** _____ around the world. Many of these dinosaurs look strange to us. Some had **3.** _____ on their heads. Others—like *Epidendrosaurus*—attacked their prey with **4.** _____ like giant knives. What was the purpose of these unusual features? And what can they tell us about dinosaurs?

The 30 cm (12-inch) *Epidendrosaurus* lived over 160 million years ago. Its remains were discovered in China.

B. Predict. Look at the pictures at the top of this page. What do you think is unusual about this dinosaur? Read the passage to check your ideas.

MYSTERY OF THE TERRIBLE HAND

1   *Whose hand is this?* Paleontologists have been **seeking** an answer for over 40 years. In the 1960s, paleontologists discovered a pair of giant arms in Ömnögovi, an area in southern Mongolia. The **length**
5   of each arm, when fully **extended**, was 2.4 meters (eight feet)! The claws were over 25 centimeters (ten inches) long. Paleontologists called the animal *Deinocheirus* (meaning "**terrible** hand").

So what did this animal look like? Paleontologists aren't sure. Scientists have **examined** the area many times. But since the original
10   discovery, they have **dug up** only a few other bones of this dinosaur.

Despite this, scientists have some ideas about *Deinocheirus*'s **appearance**. Physically, its arms and hands were similar to *ornithomimids*—a type of dinosaur that looked like a modern-day ostrich.[1] It probably used its arms for catching food. Paleontologists
15   used *Deinocheirus's* arms to **estimate** its body size. The results were amazing. *Deinocheirus* was perhaps a huge animal—almost 12 meters (40 feet) long. This is almost as big as a *T. rex*!

Other scientists have a different **opinion**. They think *Deinocheirus* was a smaller dinosaur with extremely long arms. But why would
20   a little animal need limbs[2] so long? To climb trees or to hunt for food, perhaps? "The body is a **mystery**," says Thomas Holtz, a paleontologist at the University of Maryland in the U.S. "It might not be an *ornithomimid* at all. But then what is it?" Until paleontologists find new fossil evidence, they will continue to ask this question.

---

1 An **ostrich** is a very large bird that cannot fly.
2 Your **limbs** are your arms and legs.

Multiple Choice. Choose the best answer for each question.

Purpose

1. What is the main purpose of the reading?
   a. to explain how paleontologists find dinosaur fossils
   b. to compare *T. rex* and *Deinocheirus*
   c. to talk about different dinosaur discoveries in Mongolia
   d. to describe an unusual type of dinosaur

Detail

2. Which of these can we definitely say about *Deinocheirus*?
   a. Its body was the same size as that of *T. Rex*.
   b. Scientists believe its body was very small but with very long arms.
   c. Its body was the same size as that of an ostrich.
   d. Scientists are still trying to find out the size of its body.

Paraphrase

3. In lines 9–10, it says, *But since the original discovery, they have dug up only a few other bones of this dinosaur.* What does this mean?
   a. Only a few bones were found in the original discovery.
   b. The dinosaur found in the original discovery didn't have many bones.
   c. They haven't found very many bones since the original discovery.
   d. They have found no new bones since the original discovery.

Reference

4. What does *this* refer to in line 17?
   a. *Deinocheirus'* leg bone
   b. a modern-day ostrich
   c. the length of *Deinocheirus'* arm
   d. *Deinocheirus'* body size

Main Idea

5. The main idea of the third paragraph is that *Deinocheirus* _____.
   a. may have had a very large body
   b. was a very small dinosaur
   c. was probably not an *ornithomimid*
   d. probably lived in tall trees

Vocabulary

6. What does the word *evidence* mean in line 24?
   a. information
   b. questions
   c. mysteries
   d. beliefs

Did You Know?

Also known as "Elvisaurus," *Cryolophosaurus* had a head crest that was similar to Elvis Presley's 1950s haircut.

Inference

7. Which statement would Thomas Holtz probably agree with?
   a. *Deinocheirus* was an *ornithomimid*.
   b. Scientists have a clear idea of what *Deinocheirus* looked like.
   c. *Deinocheirus* was probably larger than *T. rex*.
   d. There is still a lot we don't know about *Deinocheirus*.

Using Definitions to Find Meaning

You will often find new words and phrases in a text. Some of these may be defined in the text. Certain words signal a definition, for example, *is, means, refers to,* and *is called.* Definitions can also be set off by certain punctuation: dashes **—** , parentheses **( )**, commas **,** , or quotation marks **" "**. These may also signal extra information about people or places in the text.

For example: Dinosaurs, *which means "terrible lizards," lived millions of years ago. Ostriches, large flightless birds, live in Africa. Nessie is physically similar to a type of plesiosaur—a sea reptile with a very long neck.*

A. Completion. Complete these sentences with definitions from the box (a–d).

a. an animal with two feet **b.** the world's most complete *T. rex* skeleton
c. the length of time it lived **d.** "tyrant lizard"

1. *Tyrannosaurus* means _____ in Greek. *Rex* means "king" in Latin.

2. *T. rex* was a biped, which refers to _____. Its arms were very small.

3. Based on fossils, a *T. rex's* lifespan—_____—was about 30 years.

4. *Tyrannosaurus Sue,* _____, was found by fossil hunter Sue Hendrickson in 1990.

B. Scanning for Meaning. Use definitions in the reading on page 101 to answer these questions.

1. What is Ömnögovi?

   _____.

2. What does the name *Deinocheirus* mean?

   _____.

3. What were *ornithomimids*?

   _____.

Critical Thinking Discuss with a partner. *Deinocheirus* was discovered in Mongolia. Where do you think future dinosaur discoveries will be made? Why?

Vocabulary Practice

A. Words in Context. Complete each sentence with the correct answer.

1. If you **examine** something, you _____.
   a. look at it quickly
   b. study it closely

2. A **mystery** is something you _____ explain.
   a. can
   b. cannot

3. An example of an **opinion** is _____.
   a. "Dinosaurs were reptiles."
   b. "Dinosaurs are very interesting."

4. If something is **terrible**, it makes you feel _____.
   a. bad or afraid
   b. happy or relaxed

5. You **dig up** something that is _____ the surface.
   a. above
   b. below

B. Completion. Complete the information using the correct form of words from the box. One word is extra.

appearance	estimate	examine	extend	length	seek

The largest ever flying animal lived 85 million years ago. It was a type of pterosaur (or "flying reptile") called *Quetzalcoatlus*. When this animal's wings were **1.** _____, each was about 12 meters (40 feet). That is the **2.** _____ of some airplanes! But did pterosaurs come from a smaller animal? And how did pterosaurs learn to fly? For years, paleontologists have been **3.** _____ answers to these questions.

Recently, one of the smallest pterosaurs was discovered in China by a team of Chinese and Brazilian paleontologists. In **4.** _____, the tiny pterosaur (called *N. crypticus*) was a small, toothless reptile with feet similar to those of a bird. Scientists **5.** _____ that *N. crypticus* lived about 120 million years ago.

> ⌄ *Quetzalcoatlus* was the largest animal ever to fly.

Word Partnership Use *opinion* with:
(*adj.*) **different** opinion, **expert** opinion, **honest** opinion, **popular** opinion; (*v.*) **ask** an opinion, **give** an opinion, **share** an opinion.

VIEWING Dinosaur Discovery

Before You Watch

A. Labeling. Label the picture using the words in the box. One word is extra. Use a dictionary to help you.

backbone	neck	rib	tail	skull	vertebrae

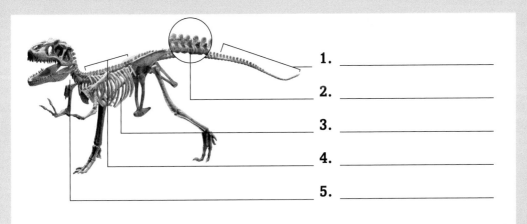

1. _____

2. _____

3. _____

4. _____

5. _____

B. Predict. Look at the video title, the map, and the picture and words in **A**. What do you think the video will be about?

Sabinas, Mexico

  a. a new dinosaur fossil that has been found

  b. new research on what dinosaurs ate

  c. how to identify dinosaur bones

While You Watch

A. True or False? Read the statements below. As you watch the video, circle whether they are **T** (true) or **F** (false).

  1. The area where the bones were found used to be a desert.   **T**   **F**

  2. Juan Pablo Garcia found the Sabinasaurio bones by accident.   **T**   **F**

  3. This is the first time that fossils have been found in the area.   **T**   **F**

  4. Local people hope that more dinosaur lovers will visit their region.   **T**   **F**

B. Matching. Check (✓) the caption that correctly describes each picture.

☐ Jose Gonzalez talks about who found the dinosaur fossils.

☐ Jose Gonzalez describes the dinosaur's size.

☐ Daniel Guajardo Ortega asks someone if he has found a fossil.

☐ Daniel Guajardo Ortega sells his fossil discovery to a scientist.

☐ This could be the most complete dinosaur skeleton found in Latin America.

☐ Scientists are not sure how to put the dinosaur together.

☐ Too many people are now visiting the city.

☐ Local people say the dinosaur discovery has changed their city.

After You Watch

Critical Thinking. Discuss these questions in a group.

1. How do you think the discovery has changed the city of Sabinas?

2. What do you think should happen to the dinosaur bones found in Sabinas?

3. What would you do if you found a fossil?

8

STORIES AND STORYTELLERS

Neuschwanstein Castle, a nineteenth-century hill top palace in Bavaria, Germany, was the inspiration for the castle in Disney's *Sleeping Beauty*.

Warm Up

Discuss these questions with a partner.

1. What is one of your favorite books or stories? Why do you like it?

2. Describe a popular author. What has he or she written? Why do you think he or she is popular?

3. Can you name a traditional story from your country?

Before You Read

Predict. Use the map, headings, and caption to answer the questions. Then read the passage to check your answers.

1. Who were the Brothers Grimm?
2. What kind of stories did they write?
3. Who were their stories for?

THE BROTHERS GRIMM

1 Jacob and Wilhelm Grimm were two young men from Germany who loved a good story. As university students, they became interested in folktales—traditional stories that people **memorized** and told again and again. They began to **collect** traditional folktales
5 from storytellers all over Germany. Many were similar to stories told in France, Italy, Japan, and other countries. Between 1812 and 1814, the brothers **published** two books in German. These included stories like "Hansel and Gretel" and "Little Red Riding Hood." The collections became known in English as *Grimm's Fairy Tales*.

10 ## Darkness and Magic

The Grimm brothers' tales **reflected** traditional life and beliefs. For example, forests are common in Germany, and this image often appears in the Grimms' stories. In the past, many people believed forests were dangerous places. In the Grimms' stories, a forest is the
15 home of evil witches, talking animals, and other **magical** beings.

Children's stories?

Although most people today think of these stories as fairy tales for children, the brothers first wrote them **primarily** for adults. Many of their early tales were dark and a little **scary**. Later, the brothers
20 changed the **text** of some of the original stories. They "softened" many of the tales and added drawings. This made them more **appropriate** for children. Like the early tales, though, each story still has a moral: work hard, be good, and listen to your parents.

Today, the Grimms' tales, such as "Red Riding Hood," are read and enjoyed in over 160 languages.

Germany

Reading Comprehension

Multiple Choice. Choose the best answer for each question.

Purpose

1. What is the main purpose of the reading?
   a. to compare the Grimms' stories to modern children's stories
   b. to explain why storytelling is important in Germany
   c. to examine two of the Grimms' fairy tales
   d. to give information about the Grimm brothers and their stories

Reference

2. What does *many* refer to in line 5?
   a. folktales and traditional stories
   b. books
   c. published collections
   d. the histories of different countries

Detail

3. Which of these is true about the Grimm brothers?
   a. They invented the fairy tales in their books.
   b. They wrote their books in different languages.
   c. They became interested in folktales as students.
   d. They traveled to many countries to collect stories.

Main Idea

4. What would be a good title for the second paragraph?
   a. The Grimms' Lives Change
   b. Tales of the Forest
   c. The First Fairy Tale
   d. Belief in Magical Beings

Reference

5. In line 21, what does *them* refer to?
   a. the Grimm brothers
   b. the children
   c. the fairy tales
   d. the adults

Vocabulary

6. In line 23, what does *moral* mean?
   a. interest
   b. text
   c. story
   d. message

Detail

7. Which of these is true about the Grimms' stories?
   a. The later stories had morals, like the early ones.
   b. The early stories were written for children.
   c. The early stories had a lot of drawings.
   d. The later stories reflected German life, but the early ones didn't.

Did You Know?

In the darker version of the story "Cinderella," the evil stepsisters cut off their toes so they could wear the glass slipper.

Annotating Text

As you read a passage in detail, it may be useful to mark—or annotate—the text. This allows you to focus on the most important information, and to remember it later. Here are some ways to add annotations:

- Use one or more colors to highlight the main ideas or most important parts.
- Underline new words and write their definitions in the margins.
- Put a circle around important numbers, statistics, or dates.
- Put a question mark (?) next to things you don't understand, for checking later.

A. Annotating. Look at the annotated paragraph from "The Brothers Grimm." Then annotate the rest of the reading on page 108.

Jacob and Wilhelm Grimm were two young men from Germany who loved a good story. As university students, they became interested in folktales—traditional stories that people memorized and told again and again. They began to collect traditional folktales from storytellers all over Germany. *< people who write or tell stories* Many were similar to stories told in France, Italy, Japan, and other countries. Between (1812) and (1814) the brothers published two books. These included stories like *"Hansel and Gretel"* and *"Little Red Riding Hood." ?*

B. Summarizing. Look back at your annotated text on page 108. Then complete the information.

collected tales from German
1. _____

origin of the stories

stories are **2.** _____ to tales in other countries

Grimms' Fairy Tales

common image

the **3.** _____

their readers

wrote first for **4.** _____ and later for **5.** _____

Critical Thinking Discuss with a partner. Do you think it was right for the Grimm brothers to "soften" their stories? Why or why not? What folktales and fairy tales do you know from your country? What kind of morals do they have?

Vocabulary Practice

A. Completion. Complete the passage by circling the correct word in each pair.

In Finland, there once was an area known as Viena Karelia. The people there were great storytellers and had many folktales and legends. The most famous is the *Kalevala*. This is a **1. (collection / text)** of several poems that forms one long story. The *Kalevala* tells tales of **2. (magical / appropriate)** beings and **3. (scary / published)** monsters.

For centuries, storytellers, called *rune singers*, have learned and spoken the *Kalevala* from memory. Today, Jussi Huovinen is Finland's last great rune singer. When he dies, the ancient culture of singing the *Kalevala* will come to an end because no one has **4. (reflected / memorized)** the entire *Kalevala*.

Finland

But there is good news. **5. (Primarily / Although)** Jussi Houvinen is the last rune singer, many of the *Kalevala's* ideas will not die with him. British author J.R.R. Tolkien (who wrote *The Lord of the Rings*) **6. (published / appropriate)** several stories in which many of the *Kalevala's* ideas are **7. (magical / reflected)**. Some characters in Tolkien's books also speak a language similar to the ancient Finnish language used in the *Kalevala*.

▽ "The Curse of Kullervo," a scene from the *Kalevala*

B. Matching. Match the correct forms of words in **red** from **A** with the correct definitions.

1. _____: any written material

2. _____: mainly, mostly

3. _____: making you feel afraid

4. _____: despite

5. _____: right for a particular person or situation

6. _____: a set or group of something

7. _____: to show (e.g., in a mirror)

8. _____: to learn something so you remember it exactly

> **Word Link** We can add **-en** to some adjectives to form verbs. For example, if you *soften* something, you make it soft. Other examples are: *darken*, *sharpen*, *weaken*.

Before You Read

A. Discussion. Read this first paragraph of a story. Then answer the questions below.

1   Once upon a time, there lived a man and a woman who had seven sons. The couple wanted a daughter very much, and, eventually, they had a girl. She was very pretty, and her parents loved her very much. One day, the father needed water for the child, so he sent the seven brothers to a
5   well in the forest to get it. Once there, though, the boys began to fight and the water jug fell into the well . . .

    1. How many children did the couple have?

    2. Why were the brothers in the forest?

    3. What happened there?

B. Predict. What do you think happens next in the story? Read lines 7–15 on the next page to check your ideas. How do you think the story ends? Read the rest of the story to find out.

THE TALE OF THE
SEVEN RAVENS

. . . The **youths** looked into the well and thought of their father. They were afraid to go home.

Hours passed. "Where are those boys?" shouted the
10 father angrily. "They are probably playing a game and have forgotten about the water. I wish they were all turned into ravens!" And when he looked up, he saw seven black birds flying away. The father was **shocked**. "What have I done?" he thought. But it was too late. He could not
15 take back his words.

In time, the girl grew up and discovered she had brothers. The story of their misfortune[1] **affected** her **deeply**, and she decided to find them. For years, she searched and did not stop. She was **determined** to find them. Finally, she
20 found their home. To enter, she needed a special key made from a chicken bone, which she did not have. The girl thought for a moment, and then took a knife and cut off one of her fingers. With it, she opened the front door and went inside. On a table, there were seven plates and seven
25 cups. She ate and drank a little from each of them. In the last cup, she **accidentally** dropped a ring that her parents had given her.

Eventually, the ravens returned for their meal. The girl **hid** behind the door and watched. When the seventh raven
30 drank from his cup, something hit his mouth. The raven **recognized** it **immediately**—it was his parents' ring. "I wish our sister were here," he said, "and then we could be free." At that moment, their sister ran to them, and **suddenly** the ravens were human again. The brothers
35 kissed their sister, and all eight of them went home together happily.

---

1 **Misfortune** is bad luck.

Reading Comprehension

Multiple Choice. Choose the best answer for each question.

Gist
1. What is this story mainly about?
   a. a father who leaves his children
   b. a bad witch who lives in a forest
   c. a sister who saves her brothers
   d. magical birds that help children

Vocabulary
2. In lines 11–12, what does *turned into* mean?
   a. changed to
   b. be interested in
   c. circled around
   d. returned to

Paraphrase
3. What does *He could not take back his words* (lines 14–15) mean?
   a. He could not remember what he had said.
   b. He had already said the words, so it was too late.
   c. He could not find the right thing to say.
   d. He was too surprised to say anything else.

Detail
4. Why does the girl cut off her finger?
   a. so she can remove a ring
   b. because her finger is stuck in a door hole
   c. because she needs it to change her brothers back
   d. so she can use it to enter the ravens' house

Sequence
5. What is the first thing the girl does when she enters the ravens' house?
   a. She takes out a knife.
   b. She hides behind a door.
   c. She eats and drinks.
   d. She sits and waits for the ravens to return home.

Detail
6. How do the ravens become human again?
   a. Their sister kisses them.
   b. They eat a magic ring.
   c. One raven makes a wish after seeing his parents' ring.
   d. They drink from a special cup that belonged to their father.

Inference
7. What lesson is taught in this story?
   a. Your parents always know best.
   b. Think carefully about what you say.
   c. Don't talk to strange people.
   d. Work hard and you will be happy.

Did You Know?

There are many folktales about animals changing into humans. In Japanese stories, clever fox spirits can turn into beautiful women to trick people.

Understanding Pronoun Reference

Pronouns are words such as *he, she, they,* and *them,* and usually refer to a noun earlier in a text. Writers use them when they don't want to repeat the same names or words over and over again. To fully understand a text, it is important to know what each pronoun refers to. Notice that pronouns match the *gender* and *number* of the noun.

The father needed water. He sent the brothers to a well to get it. Once there, they began to fight.

A. Matching. Read the summary of the fairy tale "Hansel and Gretel." Then draw an arrow to the word or phrase each underlined pronoun refers to.

A poor man and his wife had two children named Hansel and Gretel. Their mother died when **1.** they were young. Their father married again—to a terrible woman who became their stepmother. One day, **2.** she took the children into the forest and left **3.** them there. But Hansel had some bread in his pocket and dropped pieces of **4.** it on the path so that they could find their way home. However, birds ate all the bread. The children were lost!

After walking for a long time, Hansel and Gretel saw a house made of chocolate, candies, and cake. They broke off a piece of **5.** it and started to eat. An old woman opened the door and let them in. **6.** She gave them food and let them stay in the house. But this old woman was a witch. **7.** She wanted to make the children fatter so she could cook and eat **8.** them!

One day, Hansel and Gretel escaped. They pushed the witch into the oven and shut **9.** it. When they got home, they learned that their stepmother had died. Hansel and Gretel stayed with their father, and **10.** they all lived happily ever after.

B. Reference. Find these sentences in the reading on pages 112 and 113. Write the word each underlined pronoun refers to.

1. She was very pretty, and her parents loved her very much. (line 3) _____
2. With it, she opened the front door and went inside. (lines 23–34) _____
3. She ate and drank a little from each of them. (line 25) _____

Critical Thinking Discuss with a partner. Do you think the father behaved badly in "The Tale of the Seven Ravens?"

Vocabulary Practice

A. Words in Context. Complete each sentence with the correct answer.

1. If something happens **accidentally**, it happens _____.

   a. without you planning it   b. because you planned it

2. If something happens **immediately** or **suddenly**, it happens _____.

   a. over a long period of time   b. quickly

3. If you **hide** something, you _____ people to see it.

   a. want   b. don't want

4. You **recognize** a person or thing you _____.

   a. know   b. don't know

5. If you are **shocked** by something, it surprises you—usually in a _____ way.

   a. bad   b. good

B. Completion. Complete the information with words from the box.

affect	deep	determined	youths

Sol Guy and Josh Thome are modern-day storytellers who share real-life fairy tales. In one story, a poor child grows up and helps thousands of people in East Africa. In another, a successful hip-hop artist from Brazil builds community centers and helps children. These people are **1.** _____ to make changes and improve lives. Guy and Thome's TV show, *4REAL*, tells these people's stories.

Each *4REAL* show takes a celebrity (an actor or a musician) to a different country. There, the celebrities meet **2.** _____ who are helping others. Guy and Thome hope that the stories will **3.** _____ you in a **4.** _____ way. "Once you see what [these] people are [doing], you'll never think about these issues in the same way," says Thome.

On their TV show, *4REAL*, Josh Thome and Sol Guy have worked with celebrities including actress Cameron Diaz, pictured here with school children in Boston, U.S.A.

> **Usage** *Effect* and *affect* are often confused. *Effect* is a noun; *affect* is a verb. *The earthquake affected thousands of people. / The scientist studied the effect of the new medicine on rats.*

VIEWING Sleepy Hollow

Before You Watch

A. Summary. "The Legend of Sleepy Hollow" is a famous short story by American writer Washington Irving. Look at the painting below, read the caption, and complete the summary using the words in **bold**.

Long ago, in a place called Sleepy Hollow, there was a teacher named Ichabod Crane. He wanted to marry a girl named Katrina Van Tassel. But so did another man called Brom Bones.

One night, Ichabod rode on his horse to a party at the Van Tassels' home. Brom Bones was there as well. On his way home, Ichabod saw something very scary—a _____ horseman. The horseman was holding a _____ with a face cut into it—a jack-o-lantern. The horseman started to chase Ichabod. Finally, Ichabod made it across a _____ by the church. Thinking he was safe, Ichabod looked back. The horseman was still there, and he threw the pumpkin straight at Ichabod.

No one ever saw Ichabod again. Brom Bones and Katrina Van Tassel got married, and whenever anyone told the story of Ichabod Crane and the headless horseman, Brom Bones would just smile.

∧ This painting by John Quidor depicts a scene from "The Legend of Sleepy Hollow" showing the **Headless** Horseman throwing a **pumpkin** at Ichabod Crane, shortly after Ichabod crosses the church **bridge**.

While You Watch

A. Matching. Who says these things? Match the person to what he or she says in the video.

a. "The hardest problem is a real jack-o-lantern. We've tried that several times."

b. "So many times I ask myself, is it real or just a legend?"

c. "Now dwelling in these parts, in a tenant house, was a certain schoolmaster by the name of Ichabod Crane."

d. "And when he was writing the book, he remembered the name on the stone: Katrina Van Tassel."

☐ Jonathon Kruk, Storyteller

☐ Bill Lent, Caretaker, Old Dutch Church

☐ Carmen Cruz, Sleepy Hollow Resident

☐ Sal Tarantino, Headless Horseman

B. Completion. Complete these sentences by circling the correct word in each pair.

1. The narrator says that Sleepy Hollow today is a (**fun** / **scary**) place to visit.

2. Washington Irving wrote "The Legend of Sleepy Hollow" (**after** / **while**) he visited Sleepy Hollow.

3. Sal Tarantino finds it (**easy** / **hard**) to ride the horse while holding the jack-o-lantern.

4. Irving (**was** / **wasn't**) pleased when the train first arrived in Sleepy Hollow.

After You Watch

Storytelling. Choose a legend or folktale. Think about the setting (where and when it takes place), the characters (the people in the story), and the main events. Take notes. Then tell your story to a partner. Answer any questions your partner has.

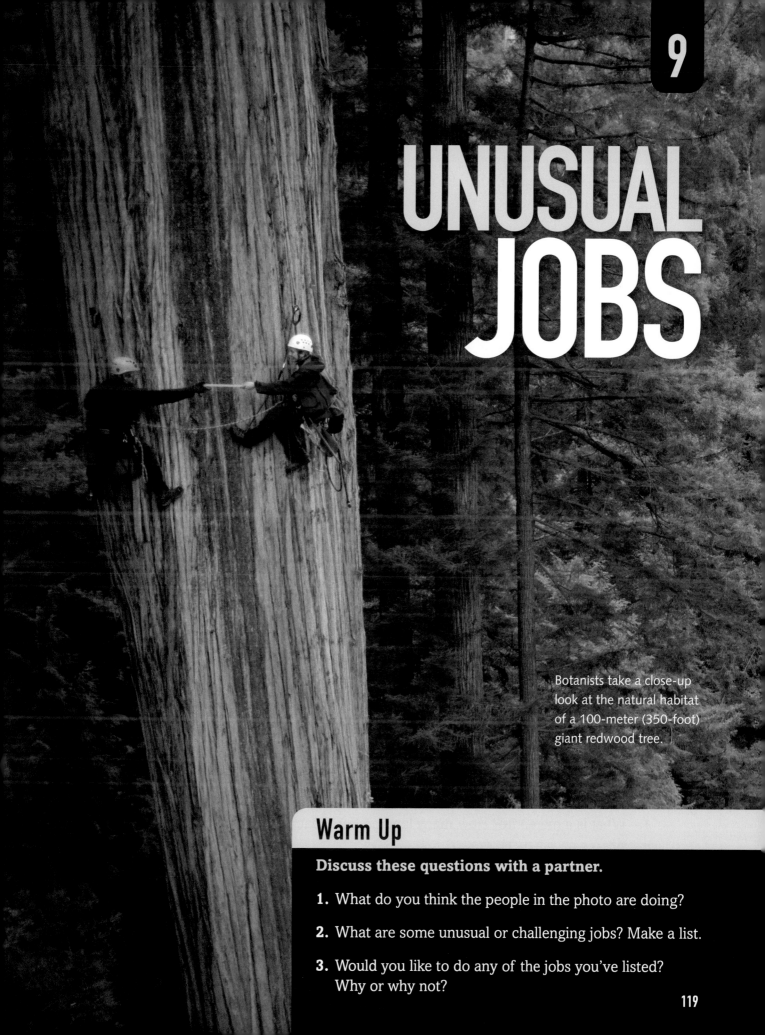

9

UNUSUAL JOBS

Botanists take a close-up look at the natural habitat of a 100-meter (350-foot) giant redwood tree.

Warm Up

Discuss these questions with a partner.

1. What do you think the people in the photo are doing?

2. What are some unusual or challenging jobs? Make a list.

3. Would you like to do any of the jobs you've listed? Why or why not?

119

Before You Read

This meteorite fell from the sky over Russia in 2013 and broke into many pieces. Originally, it was about 15 meters (50 feet) long and weighed about 10,000 metric tons.

A. Discussion. Read the paragraph. Then answer the questions below.

A meteorite is a piece of rock or metal from space. Hundreds of small meteorites fall to Earth each year and cause no problems. But large ones sometimes land, too, and these can be dangerous. Scientists are interested in meteorites because they can teach us about space and our own planet. Some are also filled with important metals like iron and gold.

1. What is a meteorite? How many land on Earth each year?
2. What can people learn from meteorites?

B. Skim and Predict. Look quickly at the interview on pages 121–122, and answer the questions below. Then read the passage to check your ideas.

1. What is Michael Farmer's job? What does he do, exactly?
2. What do you think are the challenging parts of his job?

MEET THE METEORITE HUNTER

1 *Michael Farmer is a meteorite hunter. Here, he talks about his unusual job.*

National Geographic: What's the hardest part of your job?

5 **Michael Farmer:** I'm always looking for new pieces [of meteorite rock], so I have to travel a lot. I've been to about 70 countries or so. The job can be dangerous because some rocks are worth a lot. On one such trip, I was robbed and almost killed. That was scary.

10 There are other issues, too. It's **illegal** to take meteorite pieces from some countries. So you have to be very careful and learn the **law**. It's different everywhere.

Michael Farmer looks for meteorite pieces. Some are worth thousands of dollars.

NG: Are there a lot of meteorite pieces on Earth?

15 **Michael Farmer:** Yes, there are millions, but most land in the forest, jungle, or ocean. They're impossible to **locate**. One of the best places to find pieces is in the Sahara Desert in Africa. You can see them easily in the sand. The heat also **preserves** the rocks well.

20 **NG:** What's the most valuable meteorite you found?

Michael Farmer: I found one piece in the Middle East, and I sold it for $100,000. It was a small piece—about the size of a walnut. But the most **valuable** was in Canada. Three partners and I discovered a very **rare** type of meteorite called 25 a pallasite. It **weighed** 53 kilos (117 pounds), and it's around 4.5 billion years old. We sold it to the Canadian government for just under a million dollars. Now it's in the Royal Ontario Museum in Toronto. It's a national **treasure**.

NG: Who else buys the rocks from you?

30 **Michael Farmer:** Museums and private **collectors** are always calling me. New meteorites are **in demand**, and so they sell quickly. I also sell them to a lot of scientists. They don't have the time or money to search for these rocks. Without the help of hunters, 99 percent of these meteorites 35 would be lost to science.

" Without the help of hunters, 99 percent of these meteorites would be lost to science."

This 2,200 kg (4,800 pound) iron-nickel meteorite was found in the Empty Quarter, Saudi Arabia.

Reading Comprehension

Multiple Choice. Choose the best answer for each question.

Purpose

1. What is the main purpose of this reading?
   a. to describe an unusual job
   b. to understand where meteorites come from
   c. to explain how anyone can find meteorites
   d. to find out what is difficult about hunting meteorites

Detail

2. What does Farmer say is difficult about his job?
   a. keeping meteorites safe
   b. traveling to find meteorites
   c. selling meteorites
   d. preserving meteorites

Paraphrase

3. In lines 12–13, Farmer says, *It's different everywhere.*
   What does he mean?
   a. Different countries have different meteorites.
   b. Different countries have different laws.
   c. Different countries have different safety measures.
   d. There are different laws for certain kinds of meteorites.

Detail

4. Why is the Sahara Desert a good place to find meteorites?
   a. The sand makes it easy to spot them.
   b. Most meteorites land there.
   c. Meteorites found there are rare.
   d. Meteorites there are bigger than elsewhere.

Detail

5. Where did Farmer find a meteorite worth about a million dollars?
   a. the Sahara Desert
   b. the Middle East
   c. Canada
   d. Russia

Paraphrase

6. What does the phrase *New meteorites are in demand* in line 31 mean?
   a. Meteorites are popular among collectors.
   b. Meteorites are easily available to collectors.
   c. Meteorites are rare, and so collectors can't buy them.
   d. Meteorites are valuable to collectors.

Did You Know?

Pallasites are extremely rare. Only 61 have been found, including ten in Antarctica.

Reference

7. In line 32, what does *they* refer to?
   a. scientists
   b. museums
   c. hunters
   d. new meteorites

Identifying Exact vs. Approximate Numbers

A writer may use exact numbers (e.g., *at noon, a hundred years ago, 50 percent*) in a text if he or she is sure of the facts or if it is important to give a specific figure. The writer may also provide approximate numbers (*around noon, almost a hundred years ago, nearly 50 percent*) if he or she isn't sure or if it is better to provide a larger range. These words indicate a number that is not exact but approximate: *about, around, approximately, nearly, almost, (just) under/over, circa,* and *. . . or so.*

A. Noticing. Read the following text. Circle the exact numbers. Underline the approximate numbers.

> In 2011, a meteorite from Mars was found in the Sahara Desert. Nicknamed "Black Beauty," the baseball-sized meteorite weighs just over 300 grams.
>
> A hundred or so meteorites from Mars have been found on Earth. At around 2.1 billion years old, Black Beauty is the second-oldest Martian meteorite ever found on Earth.
>
> After over a year of study, scientists found that Black Beauty contains approximately ten times the amount of water as other Martian meteorites. Scientists say this shows that Mars was warmer and wetter than previously believed.

B. Completion. Look back at the reading and captions on pages 120–122. Answer the questions with exact or approximate numbers.

1. When did the meteorite land in Russia? _____
2. How much did it originally weigh? _____
3. How many countries has Michael Farmer traveled to? _____
4. What was the selling price for the meteorite Farmer found in the Middle East? _____
5. How old was the pallasite that Farmer and his team found? _____
6. How much did the pallasite weigh? _____

Critical Thinking Discuss with a partner. Do you think people who find meteorites should be allowed to sell them? Why or why not? What would you do if you found a meteorite?

Vocabulary Practice

A. Completion. Complete the information with the correct form of words from the box. One word is extra.

| collect | illegal | in demand | law | valuable | weighed |

Unusual Jobs That Pay Well

We all know that doctors and lawyers make good money. But what are some unusual jobs that also pay well?

A **hacker** is someone who can get into a computer system without permission. This is usually **1.** _____, but it is possible to be a hacker and not break the **2.** _____. Some companies give jobs to hackers because they can help identify problems with the company's computers.

Have you ever wondered what happens to a crime scene after the police leave? A **crime scene cleaner** comes in. These cleaners are always **3.** _____ because it is not a job anyone can do. For one thing, you need to be comfortable with blood—and sometimes dead bodies.

An **upcycler** changes trash into something more **4.** _____— something that people may pay a lot of money for. First, upcyclers need to **5.** _____ a lot of items that people no longer need—like candy wrappers or an old suitcase. Then they turn those items into things people might want to buy, like a bag or a coffee table.

∧ an upcycled water can

B. Words in Context. Complete each sentence with the correct answer.

1. If you **locate** something, you _____ it.

   a. find   b. lose

2. One way to **preserve** fruit is to _____ it.

   a. burn   b. freeze

3. A **rare** animal is _____.

   a. common   b. uncommon

4. If someone **weighs** a horse, they find out how _____ it is.

   a. heavy   b. tall

5. An example of **treasure** is _____.

   a. a set of gold coins   b. a can of paint

> **Word Link** We can add **il-** and **ir-** to some words to show an opposite meaning. For example, *illegal* means "not legal." Other examples include *irregular* and *irresponsible*.

Before You Read

A. Matching. Look at the photo and read the caption. Match the correct form of each word in **bold** with its definition.

1. not safe; able to cause harm or injury   _____
2. to set on fire   _____
3. an area of land that is 10,000 square meters   _____
4. a fire that is out of control and moves quickly   _____

B. Predict. Read the three questions in the headings on the next page. What do you think the answers are? Read the passage to check your ideas.

∧ Thousands of **wildfires** occur around the globe every year. The fires **burn** millions of **hectares** of land. Hot, dry weather and fast-moving winds often make these fires more **dangerous**.

SMOKEJUMPERS

1 Every year, wildfires **destroy** millions of hectares of forest land. Homes are damaged, and thousands of people die. Smokejumpers help to stop this.

What is a smokejumper?

5 Smokejumpers are a special type of firefighter. They jump from planes or are lowered by helicopters into areas that are difficult to reach by car or on foot, such as the **middle** of a mountain forest. They **race** to put out fires as fast as they can.

What do smokejumpers do?

10 At a fire site, smokejumpers first examine the land and decide how to fight the fire. Their main goal is to stop a fire from spreading. Using basic **equipment** such as shovels and axes,[1] smokejumpers clear land of burnable[2] material, like plants and other dry material. They carry water with them, too, but only a **limited** amount.

15 ## Who can be a smokejumper?

Although the **majority** of smokejumpers are men, more women are joining. Most important are your **height** and weight. Smokejumpers **employed** in the U.S., for example, must be 120 to 200 pounds (54 to 91 kilograms) so they don't get blown away by the strong winds
20 or get hurt when they land.

Smokejumpers must also be **capable** of surviving in the wilderness. In Russia, many smokejumpers know how to find food in the forest and even make simple furniture[3] from trees.

The work is dangerous, and the hours are long. But for these
25 firefighters, smokejumping isn't just an **occupation**. They love being able to jump out of planes, fight fires, and live in the forest. As 28-year-old Russian smokejumper Alexi Tishin says, "This is the best job for tough guys."

"We face danger three times: one when we fly; two when we jump; three when we go to [the] fire."

Valeriy Korotkov, smokejumper

---

1 A **shovel** is a tool used for digging earth; an **ax** is a tool used for cutting wood.

2 If something is **burnable**, it can start a fire easily.

3 Objects such as chairs, tables, and beds are known as **furniture**.

Reading Comprehension

Multiple Choice. Choose the best answer for each question.

Gist

1. What is the reading mainly about?
 a. the life of a Russian smokejumper
 b. who smokejumpers are and what they do
 c. the difficulties of being a female smokejumper
 d. why people become smokejumpers

Detail

2. Which of these is NOT true for smokejumpers?
 a. They get to fires from a plane or a helicopter.
 b. They put out fires in areas that are hard to reach.
 c. They must learn to survive in the wilderness.
 d. They must learn to fly planes and helicopters.

Russia

Did You Know?

Russia has more than 20,000 wildfires each year and about 4,000 smokejumpers—the largest number in the world.

Detail

3. When a smokejumper gets to a fire site, what is the first thing he or she does?
 a. looks for water
 b. clears the land
 c. starts a small fire
 d. studies the land

Detail

4. If you want to be a smokejumper, you must be _____.
 a. older than 28
 b. male
 c. within a certain weight range
 d. a university graduate

Vocabulary

5. In line 21, *surviving in the wilderness* means being able to _____.
 a. live in the outdoors
 b. jump out of planes
 c. fight fires
 d. make simple furniture

Inference

6. In Alexi Tishin's opinion, why do people become smokejumpers?
 a. for the money
 b. for the excitement
 c. to help their country
 d. to work short hours

Main idea

7. What is the main idea of the last paragraph?
 a. Smokejumpers like living in the forest.
 b. Smokejumpers are tougher than firefighters.
 c. Smokejumpers love what they do.
 d. Smokejumpers work very long hours.

Paraphrasing Sentences

When you paraphrase a sentence, you rewrite it in your own words but keep the original idea. It's an important skill for many tests in English. To write paraphrased sentences, try to change both the words and the word order.

Original: Being a smokejumper is not easy. The work is not safe.
Paraphrased: It's difficult to be a smokejumper. It's dangerous work.

Words can have more than one synonym. If you use a synonym, be sure to choose the correct one.

Original: Smokejumpers know how to *find* food.
Paraphrased: Smokejumpers are able to *locate* food. ✓
Paraphrased: Smokejumpers are able to *notice* food. ✗

A. Multiple Choice. Choose the sentence that correctly paraphrases the first.

1. A smokejumper's main goal is to stop a fire from spreading.
   a. One thing a smokejumper does is to end fires that spread.
   b. The key job of a smokejumper is to keep a fire from spreading.

2. In Russia, there are more fires than anywhere else in the world.
   a. The fires in Russia are the biggest on the planet.
   b. Russia has more fires than any other place on Earth.

3. Fast-moving winds can make fires more dangerous.
   a. Fires can become more dangerous when there are strong winds.
   b. Fires that move quickly are a result of dangerous winds.

B. Completion. Complete the second sentence so that it paraphrases the first.

1. Smokejumpers have an unusual job.
   A smokejumper's _____.

2. More men than women are smokejumpers.
   There are more _____.

3. Many people were injured by the fire.
   The fire _____.

Critical Thinking Discuss these questions with a partner. How would you describe someone who works as a smokejumper? Can you think of other jobs that are dangerous? Why do you think people decide to take these jobs?

Vocabulary Practice

A. Words in Context. Complete each sentence with the correct answer.

1. If something is **limited**, it is _____.

   a. not enough
   b. more than enough

2. If you **destroy** something, it can _____ be used again.

   a. now
   b. never

3. We measure **height** in _____.

   a. kilograms / pounds
   b. centimeters / inches

4. If a book is in the **middle** of the table, it is _____ of the table.

   a. in the center
   b. near the edge

B. Completion. Complete the information with words from the box. One word is extra.

capable	employed	equipment	majority
middle	occupation	race	

During the week, eighteen-year-old student A.J. Coston lives with his family. But on the weekend, Coston lives and works at a fire station, where he is **1.** _____ as a volunteer[1] firefighter. Several times each weekend, he has to **2.** _____ to the scene of a fire.

To get the job, Coston had to take classes and learn different safety skills. He also had to learn to use different firefighting **3.** _____—axes, special flashlights, and other tools. When Coston was **4.** _____ of using these, he was allowed to work inside burning buildings.

Although firefighters spend the **5.** _____ of their time putting out fires, they also help people who have had accidents. This, says Coston, is one of the most important parts of a firefighter's **6.** _____.

---

1 If you are a **volunteer**, you do work for free.

Word Link We can add **–ment** to some verbs to form nouns. These nouns often describe an action, a process, or a state of being (*employment, encouragement*) or an object or a place (*equipment, settlement*).

VIEWING Wildfire Photographer

Before You Watch

A. Labeling. Read the caption and label the items with the words in **bold**.

1. _____

2. _____

3. _____

4. _____

∧ Facing strong heat and thick **smoke**, *National Geographic* **photographer** Mark Thiessen has a tough hobby. Every summer, he takes his **camera**, drives out West, and spends his vacation photographing **wildfires**.

While You Watch

A. True or False? Read the statements below. As you watch the video, circle whether they are **T** (true) or **F** (false).

1. Thiessen usually takes photos of wild animals.   **T**   **F**

2. Thiessen first wanted to become a photographer when he was in college.   **T**   **F**

3. Thiessen is interested in fires because it's difficult to predict them.   **T**   **F**

4. Thiessen is also a firefighter.   **T**   **F**

5. Because it's so dangerous, Thiessen plans to stop photographing wildfires soon.   **T**   **F**

B. Matching. Check (✓) the caption that correctly describes each picture.

Mark Thiessen
National Geographic Photographer

☐ Thiessen's job is not as exciting as you might think.

☐ Thiessen's job is more exciting than you might think.

☐ A powerful wind pushes against the truck.

☐ Thiessen needs to drive away from the fire immediately.

☐ A fire whirl happens when flames twist together.

☐ The fire spreads from the ground into the trees.

☐ The sight of trees damaged by fires can be quite beautiful.

☐ There are 100,000 wildfires in the U.S. every year.

After You Watch

Critical Thinking. Discuss these questions in a group.

1. What qualities do you think are important to have as a photographer? How about as a firefighter?

2. Do you think you could be a wildfire photographer? Why or why not?

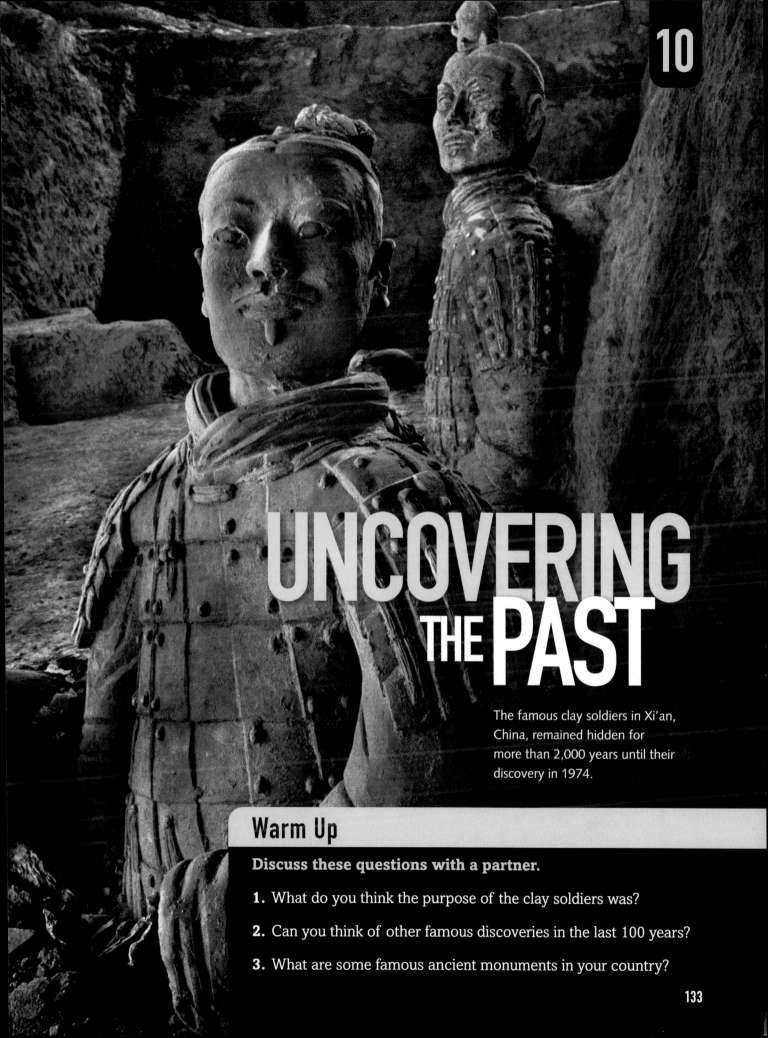

10

UNCOVERING THE PAST

The famous clay soldiers in Xi'an, China, remained hidden for more than 2,000 years until their discovery in 1974.

Warm Up

Discuss these questions with a partner.

1. What do you think the purpose of the clay soldiers was?

2. Can you think of other famous discoveries in the last 100 years?

3. What are some famous ancient monuments in your country?

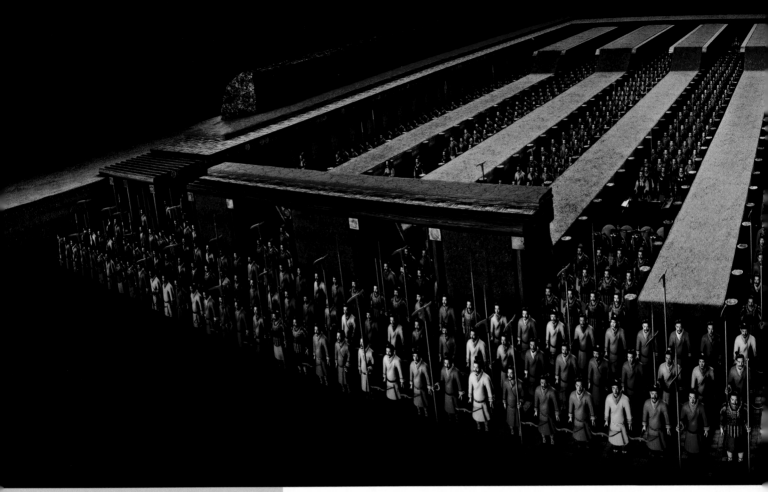

Before You Read

Warriors in the front and side rows of the Emperor's terracotta army carried long-range weapons such as crossbows. Officers, horses, and foot soldiers stood in the army's central sections.

A. Completion. Read the paragraph. Then match the words in **bold** to the correct definitions below.

Can you imagine digging in your yard one day and finding a life-sized **soldier** made completely of clay? That's what happened several decades ago when farmers in Xi'an, China, were digging wells. **Archeologists** have since found about 6,000 more of these soldiers, along with horses, weapons, tools, and other **artifacts**. The huge **army** was meant to protect the **tomb** of the first ruler of China. The image above shows how it might have originally looked.

1. _____ are scientists who study objects from the past.

2. _____ are objects that people made in the past, such as tools.

3. A(n) _____ is a person in a large fighting group, or _____.

4. A(n) _____ is a place where a dead body is kept.

B. Predict. Look at the photo on page 136. Why do you think the clay soldiers today are brown, and not in full color? Read the passage to check your ideas.

THE ARMY'S TRUE COLORS

1   The first emperor[1] of China, Qin Shihuang, **accomplished** a huge amount during his rule. Between 221 and 210 B.C., he started the **construction** of the Great Wall. He built a large **network** of roads. He introduced a new writing
5   system, **currency**, and set of measurements. The emperor also ordered the construction of a huge army of life-sized terracotta[2] soldiers. These, he hoped, would **protect** his tomb after his death.

Lost in Time

10   The soldiers in Xi'an's terracotta museum are today light brown, but they weren't always. They began as an army of red, blue, yellow, green, white, and purple. Sadly, most of the colors did not last to the present day. After being **exposed** to air during excavation,[3] the coating under the paint began to
15   fall off. The paint disappeared in less time than it takes to boil an egg, taking with it important pieces of history.

1 An **emperor** is a leader who rules a group of regions or countries.
2 **Terracotta** is dirt or clay used for pottery and building construction.
3 **Excavation** is the act of removing objects from the ground.

New Techniques

Now new **techniques** are starting to **reveal** the army's true colors. Archeologists have recently discovered an area with
20 more than a hundred soldiers. Many of these still have their painted features, including black hair, pink faces, and black or brown eyes. Chinese and German researchers have developed a special liquid to help preserve the soldiers' colors. After they find a soldier or other artifact, archeologists spray it with the
25 liquid. They then cover it in plastic.

Back to Life

Archeologists are also finding colors in the dirt around the soldiers. It's important not to disturb the dirt, so the colors won't be lost. "We are treating the earth as an artifact," says
30 archeologist Rong Bo, the museum's leading chemist. The next challenge, says Rong, is to find a way to **apply** the colors to the army again. Once that happens, artists can bring Emperor Qin's army back to life in full, **vivid** color.

More than 1,000 warriors have been unearthed in Pit 1, burial ground of the emperor's main army.

Reading Comprehension

Multiple Choice. Choose the best answer for each question.

Gist

1. What is the reading mainly about?
   a. the death of Emperor Qin
   b. how the emperor's tomb was built
   c. the original colors of the terracotta soldiers
   d. the life of soldiers under Emperor Qin

Detail

2. The terracotta soldiers were constructed to _____.
   a. show the outside world China's greatness
   b. be enjoyed by everyday people
   c. frighten China's enemies
   d. protect Emperor Qin's tomb

Main Idea

3. What is the main idea of the second paragraph?
   a. The soldiers lost their colors very quickly.
   b. The soldiers' paint fell off because of the high temperature.
   c. Visitors to the museum are not actually seeing the real soldiers.
   d. Being exposed to water is bad for the soldiers.

Detail

4. What have archeologists recently discovered?
   a. a place with over a hundred soldiers
   b. a written description of the soldiers' true colors
   c. a special liquid in the tomb to preserve the soldiers' colors
   d. a new tomb for Emperor Qin

Vocabulary

5. In line 23, what does the word *preserve* mean?
   a. identify
   b. save
   c. destroy
   d. enjoy

Reference

6. In line 25, what does *they* refer to?
   a. soldiers
   b. visitors
   c. colors
   d. archeologists

Inference

7. Which statement would Rong Bo probably agree with?
   a. The soldiers should stay in their current, brown color.
   b. Artists should be able to paint the soldiers in any color they want.
   c. Archeologists can only guess at the soldiers' original colors.
   d. We should try to restore the army's vivid colors.

Did You Know?

Each of the clay soldiers has different facial features. Emperor Qin ordered that every warrior be completely unique.

Identifying Homonyms

Homonyms are words that have the same spelling and pronunciation, but have different meanings. You can usually tell the correct definition of a word by identifying its part of speech and using the context. For example:

back (*n.*) a body part: *My **back** hurts from moving furniture the whole day.* (*adv.*) the opposite way from the one you are facing or traveling: *She took a step **back** when the dog barked at her.*

part (*n.*) a piece of something that can be combined to make a whole: *The story had many **parts** to it.* (*v.*) to leave or be separated from each other: *They were very sad to **part** after a long journey together.*

A. Definitions. Read these sentences from the reading passage. Then decide which definition matches the word in **bold**.

1. The first emperor of China, Qin Shihuang, accomplished a huge amount during his **rule**.

   a. (*n.*) a law
   b. (*n.*) a period of control

2. He built a large **network** of roads.

   a. (*n.*) a system of connected lines
   b. (*n.*) a group of people who work together

3. The soldiers in Xi'an's terracotta museum were not always **light** brown.

   a. (*adj.*) not dark
   b. (*adj.*) not heavy

4. Sadly, most of the colors did not **last** to the present day.

   a. (*adj.*) most recent or final
   b. (*v.*) continue to exist

5. Many of these still have their painted **features**, including black hair, pink faces, and black or brown eyes.

   a. (*v.*) contains something important
   b. (*pl. n.*) parts of the face

6. We are treating the **earth** as an artifact.

   a. (*n.*) land or soil
   b. (*n.*) the third planet from the sun

7. **Once** that happens, artists can bring Emperor Qin's army back to life in full, vivid color.

   a. (*adv.*) when; as soon as
   b. (*adv.*) one time only

Critical Thinking Discuss with a partner. Do you think it's a good idea to paint the soldiers again? Why or why not?

Vocabulary Practice

A. Completion. Complete the passage by circling the correct word in each pair.

The tomb of Emperor Qin Shihuang was **1. (constructed / exposed)** more than 2,000 years ago and has never been opened. This is because archeologists, as well as the Chinese government, want to **2. (apply / protect)** what lies inside it.

Many archeologists feel we don't have the **3. (currency / techniques)** right now to preserve whatever is found there. Once the artifacts are **4. (exposed / protected)** to air, they may lose their **5. (technique / vivid)** colors, much like the terracotta soldiers.

Modern tests have also **6. (accomplished / revealed)** high levels of mercury, a liquid metal, in the area. It is thought that Emperor Qin's tomb is surrounded by a **7. (currency / network)** of rivers filled with mercury, which symbolized never-ending life.

B. Words in Context. Read the sentences and circle **T** (true) or **F** (false).

1. If you **accomplish** something, you do it successfully.   T   F

2. When you **reveal** something, you keep it secret.   T   F

3. A country's **currency** refers to its money.   T   F

4. Colors that are **vivid** are very dull.   T   F

5. **Techniques** are ways of doing something using special talent or skills.   T   F

6. In a **network** of roads, the roads are connected to each other.   T   F

7. If you **apply** paint to something, you remove it.   T   F

8. If you **protect** someone, you keep the person safe.   T   F

> **Word Partnership** Use *reveal* with: (*n.*) reveal **information**, reveal **a secret**, reveal **the truth**, reveal **the reason**.

Before You Read

A. Quiz. What do you know about the Egyptian pyramids? Read the sentences below and circle **T** (True) or **F** (False). Check your answers on page 146.

1. The pyramids at Giza are older than the pyramids of Central America.   **T**   **F**

2. When they were first built, the pyramids at Giza were white.   **T**   **F**

3. The Great Pyramid of Khufu at Giza was the world's tallest structure for over 3,000 years.   **T**   **F**

B. Predict. Read the photo caption and skim the reading on the next page. Who do you think built the Giza pyramids? Circle your answer. Then read the passage to check.

   a. foreign workers

   b. foreign slaves

   c. Egyptian workers

   d. Egyptian slaves

∧ Close to the Giza pyramids (**A**), an ancient city has been unearthed (**B**). Archeologists believe the people who built the pyramids once lived there; their tombs are hidden a short distance away (**C**).

WONDERS OF EGYPT

1   For centuries, the pyramids of Giza have been **timeless** symbols of
    Egyptian culture. But who actually built them? For years, we did not know
    for sure. But archeologists recently discovered an ancient village near the
    pyramids. Close by, there was a cemetery where pyramid builders were
5   buried. From studying these places, archeologists can now **confirm** that
    the pyramids were not built by slaves or foreigners (or space aliens!).
    Ordinary Egyptians built them.

    It took about eighty years to build the pyramids. **According to**
    archeologists, about 20,000–30,000 people were **involved** in completing
10 the **task**. The workers had different **roles**. Some dug up the rock,
    some moved it, and some shaped it into **blocks**. People also worked on
    different teams, each with its own name. These teams often **competed** to
    do a job faster.

A Pyramid Builder's Life

15 Life for these workers was hard. "We can see that in their skeletons,"
    says Azza Mohamed Sarry El-Din, a scientist studying bodies found in
    the cemetery. The bones show signs of arthritis,[1] which developed from
    carrying heavy things for a long time. Archeologists have also found many
    female skeletons in the village and cemetery. The damage to their bones
20 is similar to that of the men. Their lives may have been even tougher:
    Male workers lived to age 40–45, but women to only 30–35. However,
    workers usually had enough food, and they also had medical care if they
    got sick or hurt.

    The work was challenging, but laborers were **proud** of their work. On
25 a wall in Khufu's Great Pyramid, for example, a group of workers wrote
    Friends of Khufu. "It's because they were not just building the tomb of
    their king," says Egyptian archeologist Zahi Hawass. "They were building
    Egypt. It was a national project, and everyone was a participant."[2]

---

1 **Arthritis** is an illness that causes the hands, knees, or other joints to hurt.

2 A **participant** is a person who joins a certain activity.

Reading Comprehension

Multiple Choice. Choose the best answer for each question.

Purpose   **1.** The main purpose of this reading is to describe _____.
  - a. who the pyramid builders were and what they did
  - b. how Khufu's Great Pyramid was constructed
  - c. what life was like for Egyptian kings
  - d. why Egyptian kings wanted to build pyramids

Vocabulary   **2.** What does *dug up* in line 10 mean?
  - a. took out of the ground
  - b. broke into small pieces
  - c. placed on top of each other
  - d. joined together

Detail   **3.** Which statement about building the pyramids is true?
  - a. It took over a century to complete.
  - b. Builders all did the same work.
  - c. More than 30,000 workers were involved.
  - d. Builders worked in teams.

Gist   **4.** What is the third paragraph mainly about?
  - a. how long female workers lived
  - b. information on the lives of pyramid builders
  - c. the benefits of being a male worker
  - d. men's vs. women's roles in Egyptian society

Reference   **5.** In line 20, what does *their* refer to?
  - a. archeologists
  - b. male workers
  - c. female workers
  - d. medical workers

Vocabulary   **6.** In line 24, what does the word *laborers* mean?
  - a. kings
  - b. archeologists
  - c. workers
  - d. women

Inference   **7.** What can we infer about the people who wrote "Friends of Khufu" on a wall?
  - a. They were looking for new friends.
  - b. They were pleased with their accomplishments.
  - c. They were very angry with their bosses.
  - d. They were in trouble because of their bad behavior.

Did You Know?

The Great Pyramid is made up of more than two million blocks of stone, each one weighing about 2,200 kilograms (about 2.5 tons).

Creating an Outline Summary

Creating an outline helps readers organize their thoughts. It also helps to organize large amounts of information. To create an outline, first pick out the main ideas of the text. Next, write down the subtopic—what the author says about each main idea. Lastly, write the details given about each subtopic (usually two or three).

A. Outline. Use these notes about the passage to complete the outline.

national project
teams and roles
ordinary Egyptians

30–35 years
80 years to build
medical care

arthritis
proud of work

The Pyramid Builders

1. Construction of the pyramids
   A. Built by _____
   B. Time extent and jobs

      - _____
      - 20,000–30,000 people involved
      - People worked in different _____

2. Builders' lives and attitudes
   A. Hard life
      - bones show signs of _____
      - men lived till 40–45 years, women _____
   B. Food and health
      - enough food
      - _____
   C. Attitude of laborers
      - _____
      - saw it as a _____

Critical Thinking Discuss with a partner. Does the author feel the pyramid builders were mostly positive or negative about their work? What evidence does the author give?

Vocabulary Practice

A. Completion. Complete the information by circling the correct word in each pair.

Cleopatra became queen of Egypt at age 18, when her brother became king. The couple **1. (competed / confirmed)** for control of Egypt, and Cleopatra lost. Later, two important leaders from Rome—Julius Caesar and Marc Antony—both fell in love with her. **2. (According to / Involved)** legend, Cleopatra was very beautiful. She was also apparently very smart. With the help of Caesar and Antony, she became queen and played an important **(role / block)** in Egyptian society.

But staying in power was not an easy **4. (task / role)**. Cleopatra had many enemies[1] who eventually took power from her. In the end, the queen was too **5. (ordinary / proud)** to surrender[2] and instead chose to kill herself. Her legend survived, however, and today Cleopatra remains a(n) **6. (timeless / according)** symbol of ancient Egypt.

∧ A sculpture recovered from what is thought to be Cleopatra's palace

---

1 An **enemy** is someone who wants to harm you.

2 If you **surrender**, you stop fighting and admit you have lost.

B. Completion. Use the correct form of the words in **red** in **A** to complete the definitions.

1. If something is _____, it is common or usual.

2. A(n) _____ is an activity or some kind of work you do.

3. If something is _____, it is shown to be true.

4. A(n) _____ has flat sides and is usually square or rectangular in shape.

5. If you are _____ with something, it means you are connected or concerned with that thing.

> **Word Partnership** Use **task** with: (*v.*) **complete** a task, **give someone** a task, **perform** a task; (*adj.*) **difficult** task, **easy** task, **important** task, **impossible** task, **simple** task.

VIEWING Peru's Hidden Treasure

Before You Watch

A. Matching. Read the information and match the words below with the definitions.

Tomb raiding, also known as **grave** robbing, is the act of uncovering a tomb and stealing jewelry, **pottery**, or other artifacts. Robbers can often sell these items for very high prices. This photo shows a tomb that, luckily, archeologists found before it was robbed. It shows the **remains** of a **priest** who held great power during Peru's ancient Moche civilization.

1. remains •   • a. a man who leads or performs religious ceremonies

2. priest •   • b. cups, dishes, and other objects made from baked clay

3. pottery •   • c. parts of the body that are left after a person has been dead for a long time

4. grave •   • d. a place where a dead person is buried

While You Watch

A. Noticing. Check (✓) the sentences about the Moche people that are true.

1. ☐ They lived in northern Peru.
2. ☐ They lived at the same time as the Inca.
3. ☐ They grew corn, beans, and peanuts.
4. ☐ They disappeared at the end of the tenth century.

B. Completion. Circle the word or words that best complete each caption.

The Moche people were successful farmers and (**hunters / traders**).

The archeologist says reconstructing a culture is like putting together a (**jigsaw puzzle / broken mirror**).

The warrior priest in the art is (**probably / probably not**) the same person in the tomb.

People will be able to see the tomb's artifacts in (**a museum / an art gallery**).

After You Watch

Critical Thinking. Discuss these questions with a partner.

1. Sometimes ancient artifacts are sold to private collectors. Do you think this is OK, or should they always be kept in public museums?

2. In what ways is the discovery in this video similar to and different from the other discoveries discussed in this unit?

Answers to Before You Read, page 140:

1. True. They were built over 4,000 years ago—starting in about 2550 B.C.
2. True. The top of one of the pyramids still has its white-colored covering.
3. True. It was the tallest structure for 3,800 years—until England's Lincoln Cathedral was built in about A.D. 1300.

11

LEGENDS OF THE SEA

A diver discovers a human skull underwater in the Northern Yucatan Peninsula, Mexico.

Warm Up

Discuss these questions with a partner.

1. The man in the photo discovered a skull underwater. What other things might be buried underwater?

2. Do you know any legends about the sea or sailors?

3. What are some famous underwater discoveries?

A historic tall ship sails toward the sunset.

Before You Read

A. Matching. Read the information and match each word in **bold** with its definition.

> During the Golden Age of Piracy (1660–1730), **goods** such as cloth, spices, and weapons were commonly traded between Europe, Africa, the Caribbean, and the Americas. Pirates were a common threat to **maritime** trade, especially in the Caribbean. One famous pirate **captain** was Edward Teach, also known as Blackbeard.

a. ship's leader _____ **b.** related to the sea _____
c. things that are made to be sold _____

B. Predict. What do you think pirates were really like? Read the sentences and circle **T** (true) or **F** (false). Then read the passage to check your ideas.

1. On a pirate ship, men made the ship's rules together.   **T**   **F**

2. Pirates made most of their money by stealing gold.   **T**   **F**

3. Many pirates had wooden legs or wore earrings.   **T**   **F**

PIRATES: ROMANCE AND REALITY

1 In the movies, pirates have exciting and adventurous lives. But what was life actually like for an 18th-century pirate? Which aspects of the movie pirate are real, and which are invented?

A Pirate's Life

5 While movie pirates are men in search of adventure, the **average** pirate was usually trying to escape from a difficult life. Some were ex-sailors who were treated poorly on their ships. Others were escaped slaves who wanted their **freedom**. They came from many different backgrounds. But on a pirate ship, **equality** was important. Men elected[1] their captain and
10 created the ship's rules together. The men also **divided** the **income** from stolen goods, and they shared these earnings fairly.

---

1 If you **elect** someone, you choose that person to lead.

Pirate Treasure

In movies, pirates have chests full of gold and piles of money stolen from other people. However, it was far more common for pirates to
15 **steal** things like cloth, spices, and even medicine. They often sold these things. Of course, **purchasing** stolen goods from pirates was illegal, but many people did it. Also, unlike movie pirates, real pirates didn't **bury** their money, says Cori Convertito, who works at a maritime museum in the U.S. "They blew it as soon as they could on
20 women and booze."[2]

Pirate Style

Movie pirates often wear eye patches and have wooden legs. Many real pirates also looked like this. Why? One **factor** was the poor living conditions. "Life at sea was hard and dangerous," says David
25 Moore, a maritime museum employee in the U.S. **Disease** was also common. For these reasons, some pirates lost eyes and legs. But many pirates did one thing for their health: They wore earrings—just like in the movies. They believed putting weight on the ears stopped seasickness.

---

2 **Booze** is an informal word meaning *alcohol*.

"Duel on the Beach," by N. C. Wyeth (1882–1945), a romantic image of pirates' adventurous lives

Reading Comprehension

Multiple Choice. Choose the best answer for each question.

Main Idea

1. What is the main idea of this reading?
   a. A pirate's life was a dangerous but exciting adventure.
   b. Some things we've seen or read about pirates are true, but others aren't.
   c. The lives of 18th-century pirates and modern-day pirates are similar.
   d. Today's stories and movies about pirates are entirely wrong.

Vocabulary

2. In line 2, *aspects* is closest in meaning to _____.
   a. parts
   b. roles
   c. lives
   d. people

Detail

3. On pirate ships, _____.
   a. men were treated like slaves
   b. there were several captains
   c. only ex-sailors were allowed
   d. the men shared the money they made

Vocabulary

4. In lines 19–20, *They blew it* means
   "They _____ the money."
   a. hid
   b. spent
   c. made
   d. saved

Did You Know?

The fearsome pirate Blackbeard was said to wear burning ropes in his long beard in battle.

Inference

5. Which statement would David Moore probably agree with?
   a. Many pirates had a difficult life and probably died young.
   b. The appearance of movie pirates is very different from reality.
   c. A pirate's life wasn't as dangerous as we see in the movies.
   d. Many pirates were friendlier than we see in the movies.

Reference

6. In line 26, what does *For these reasons* refer to?
   a. the dangers of seasickness
   b. eye patches and wooden legs
   c. stealing and selling goods illegally
   d. poor living conditions and disease

Detail

7. According to the passage, pirates believed wearing earrings _____.
   a. was fashionable
   b. stopped seasickness
   c. brought good luck
   d. was only for women

Reading Skill

Finding Similarities and Differences

Writers often compare and contrast ideas. When you compare, you focus on similarities. Words that signal similarities include *like, also, as well, both, neither.* When you contrast, you focus on differences. Words that signal differences include *unlike, but, however, while.* Venn diagrams are a useful way to present this information visually.

A. Classification. Look back at the passage on pages 149–150. Match each answer (a–f) with the type of pirate it describes.

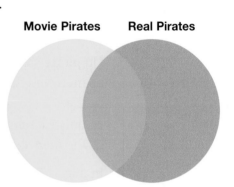

a. became pirates to have an adventure

b. wore earrings

c. mostly stole money and gold

d. sold their stolen goods and spent their earnings

e. buried their treasure

f. stole things like food and medicine

B. Completion. Now read the following passage. Underline the words that signal similarities and differences. Then complete the Venn diagram below.

Privateers are often confused with pirates because both attacked ships. However, there are differences. Pirates were basically maritime criminals who broke laws and terrified people. Privateers, however, were usually given orders by their country to attack enemy ships. Pirates usually kept everything they stole, while privateers gave part of it to their government. Life at sea was very difficult, however, so neither privateers nor pirates had easy lives.

a. attacked ships

b. broke the law

c. gave some of their money to their government

d. kept all the things they stole

e. had difficult lives

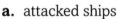 **Critical Thinking** Discuss with a partner. Think about how pirates are shown in movies. Based on the reading, in what ways are movie pirates' lives "romantic"?

Vocabulary Practice

A. Completion. Complete the passage by circling the correct word in each pair.

Most people earn a(n) **1. (disease / income)** by going to work. Not Barry Clifford. He makes money by finding lost pirate treasure. In 1984, he discovered a pirate ship called the *Whydah*, an English slave ship, in waters near Massachusetts in the U.S. It traveled to Africa, where the ship's captain **2. (buried / purchased)** a number of slaves—people who had lost their **3. (freedom / income)**. The ship then traveled to the Caribbean. Captain Sam Bellamy and his pirates took the *Whydah* and **4. (stole / purchased)** all of its goods. Later, Bellamy's men **5. (divided / averaged)** the goods among themselves. But their luck didn't last, and soon the *Whydah* sank in a storm near Massachusetts.

Today, **6. (equality / factors)** such as bad weather and rough water make it difficult for Clifford's team to bring objects up from the *Whydah*. Despite this, over 200,000 objects have been found. These discoveries have helped change our image of pirates. For example, from the pirates' clothes, scientists have learned that the **7. (divided / average)** pirate was only about 1.6 meters (5'4") tall.

B. Definitions. Use the correct form of the words in **red** from **A** to complete the definitions.

1. If you have a(n) _____, you have an illness.

2. When there is _____, all people are treated the same.

3. _____ are reasons for or causes of something.

4. If something is _____, it is put in the ground and covered with earth.

5. _____ is money you earn, usually for work you do.

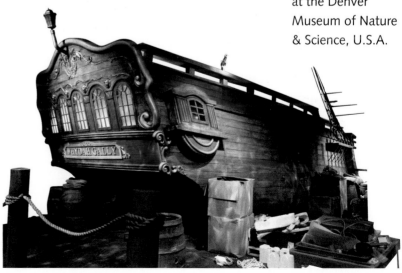

˅ A replica of the *Whydah* ship at the Denver Museum of Nature & Science, U.S.A.

> **Word Link** We can add **-dom** to some words to make nouns, meaning a state or condition. For example, *freedom* means "living in a free condition." Other examples include *boredom* and *wisdom*.

Before You Read

A. Completion. Read the information and complete the definitions below.

The Golden Age of Piracy produced a number of famous pirates. While piracy is mainly seen as an activity for men, a minority of the pirates were actually fierce women, with a **fleet** of ships of their own. One such terrifying pirate, who **attacked** boats and stole goods, was an English woman named Charlotte De Berry. Berry started her pirate career when she cut off the head of a cruel captain, who was also her husband, and **captured** his ship.

1. If you **attack** a person or thing, you try to (hurt / help) them.

2. A **fleet** is an organized group of (ships / people).

3. If you **capture** something or someone, you (take / free) it.

B. Predict. On the next page, look at the title and headings, and read the first sentence of each paragraph. Answer the questions below. Then read the passage to check your answers.

1. Why do you think the women became pirates?

2. What do you think happened to them?

Keira Knightly plays a female pirate named Elizabeth Swann in the movie *Pirates of the Caribbean.*

WOMEN OF THE WAVES

1 Throughout history, the majority of pirates have been men.
But were there any women pirates? Absolutely! Below are
two from different parts of the world.

Mary Read: Pirate in Disguise

5 Mary Read was born in England around 1690. She lived most of
her life disguised as a man. As a teenager, looking for adventure,
she dressed as a boy and got a job at sea. Later, as a young
woman (still **pretending** to be a man), she found work
on a ship and **sailed** to the Caribbean.

10 On one journey, pirates attacked Mary's ship. Instead
of fighting, she joined them. But Mary had to be careful
because many pirate ships had a rule: No women allowed.
If the men discovered her true identity, they might **shoot**
and kill her. So at first, Mary stayed by herself and **avoided**
15 the others. But soon, she made a surprising discovery:
One of the pirates on the ship was actually a woman!
Anne Bonny was the captain's girlfriend, but she was also
a pirate herself. Mary told Anne her secret, and the two
women became good friends, and powerful fighters.
20 They fought together until they were captured in 1720.

∧ Mary Read

Ching Shih: Pirate Queen

In the early 1800s, pirate Ching Shih **terrorized** the Chinese
coast. When her powerful pirate husband died, control of his
500 junks[1] **transferred** to Ching Shih. While she was in charge,
25 she expanded her fleet to almost 2,000 ships.

A **fearless** fighter, Ching Shih led nearly 80,000 pirates—
both men and women. They **targeted** ships and towns along
the coast of China. For years, leaders throughout the region
failed to stop her. Eventually, Ching Shih retired, a rich and
30 **respected** woman.

---

1 A **Junk** is a traditional type of Chinese sailing ship.

Reading Comprehension

Multiple Choice. Choose the best answer for each question.

Purpose

1. What is the main purpose of this reading?
   a. to describe two female pirates
   b. to compare male and female pirates
   c. to describe the challenges that pirates faced
   d. to show that female pirates were very common

Vocabulary

2. Look at the word *disguised* in line 6. Here, *disguise*
   means to _____.
   a. wear beautiful clothes
   b. change your appearance
   c. hide your feelings
   d. look for adventure

Reference

3. In line 15, what does *others* refer to?
   a. ships
   b. pirates
   c. women
   d. rules

Did You Know?

This 1,400 kg (3,000 pound) anchor was recovered from Blackbeard's ship. It had been underwater since 1718.

Detail

4. What unusual discovery did Mary Read make?
   a. The captain was a woman.
   b. Women weren't allowed on pirate ships.
   c. The captain was her father.
   d. Another pirate was actually a woman.

Paraphrase

5. In lines 22–23, what does *Ching Shih terrorized the Chinese coast* mean?
   a. Ching Shih took control of the Chinese coast.
   b. Ching Shih created fear among people on the Chinese coast.
   c. Ching Shih bought all the ships on the Chinese coast.
   d. Ching Shih attacked everyone who tried to leave the Chinese coast.

Detail

6. Which statement about Ching Shih's ships is NOT true?
   a. All of the sailors were women.
   b. There were about 2,000 of them.
   c. Both male and female pirates worked on them.
   d. There were almost 80,000 people on them.

Detail

7. Who was married to a pirate?
   a. Mary Read
   b. Ching Shih
   c. both Mary Read and Ching Shih
   d. neither Mary Read nor Ching Shih

Using Context to Guess the Meaning of Words

When you find a new word, look at the context—the words around it—to help you guess its meaning. First, identify the word's part of speech (noun, verb, etc.) and any suffixes and prefixes. In the sentence below, you can see *contemporary* is followed by a noun. This suggests that it could be an adjective. You can also see that it's contrasted with the earlier part of the sentence. The first adjective is *older* and so you may be able to guess that *contemporary* is its antonym, and means *current* or *modern*.

Older views of pirates were often very different from those of **contemporary** authors.

A. Multiple Choice. Find these words in the reading on page 155. Identify the part of speech, look at the context, and choose the best meaning of the word.

1. *absolutely* (line 2): a. yes   b. no   c. maybe
2. *identity* (line 13): a. weapon   b. rule   c. self
3. *expanded* (line 25): a. traveled   b. increased   c. died
4. *retired* (line 29):   a. disguised   b. became poor   c. stopped working

B. Matching. Read about another famous pirate. Guess the meaning of the **bold** words from context. Match them with their definitions.

One of the most famous pirates of all time was Captain Kidd. Born in Scotland in 1654, William Kidd actually started out as a privateer and a pirate hunter. He was hired to **apprehend** pirates and did this for many years. However, he **switched** sides to become a pirate himself. On January 30, 1698, Kidd took his greatest prize, an Armenian ship called the *Quedagh Merchant*, after a bloody **battle**. He was ordered to bring the stolen **loot** back to England. Instead, he left the ship in the Caribbean and sailed to New York on another ship. He was soon arrested and hanged in 1701.

1. apprehend   •   •   a. to catch
2. switch   •   •   b. to change
3. battle   •   •   c. treasure
4. loot   •   •   d. fight

Critical Thinking Discuss with a partner. What kinds of adventure do today's teenagers look for? In what ways are the dreams of modern teenagers different from/similar to those of teenagers in Mary's time?

Vocabulary Practice

A. Completion. Complete the information with the correct form of words from the box. One word is extra.

avoid	fearless	pretend	sail	shoot	target	transfer

Even today, pirates are common in places such as the Strait of Malacca in Southeast Asia. As it is the world's most important shipping region, about 70,000 cargo ships **1.** _____ through this area every year. Like 18th-century pirates, many of today's pirates are **2.** _____ killers, but now they have better weapons and faster boats. They mostly **3.** _____ cargo ships— for both goods and money. Some things today's pirates steal (and resell) are oil, wood, animals, and weapons.

Modern-day pirates sometimes **4.** _____ to be a boat in trouble and stop in front of a cargo ship. The cargo ship slows down to **5.** _____ hitting the boat. This gives the pirates a chance to climb onto the ship. The pirates sometimes capture people and say they will **6.** _____ the people if they don't get money.

> **Word Link** The prefix **trans-** means movement or change, e.g. *transfer, transport, transatlantic.*

B. Words in Context. Read the sentences and circle **T** (true) or **F** (false).

1. If you **terrorize** someone, you make them fear you. **T** **F**

2. If police **fail** to catch a killer, they are successful in catching him. **T** **F**

3. If you **respect** someone, you like and think highly of them. **T** **F**

4. If you **transfer** from one bus to another, you change buses. **T** **F**

⌄ Pirate attacks are still common today in the Strait of Malacca.

THAILAND
100°E
Teluk Ewa Jetty ◆ Langkawi ─PROPOSED OIL PIPELINE
Pinang
M A L A Y S I A
● Pirate attacks, 2002 through June 2007
◆ Port
Lumut
Port Kelang
Kuala Lumpur ★
Malacca
SINGAPORE
Johor Bahru
Tanjung Pelepas
105°
Nagoya
RIAU
ARCHIPELAGO
Batam
Babi Island
Tanjung Batu
S T R A I T   O F   M A L A C C A
I N D O N E S I A
25 attacks
─19 attacks
Dumai
Belawan
A C E H
S U M A T R A
North
Sungsang

ASIA CHINA
Hong Kong
INDIA
PACIFIC OCEAN
Strait of Malacca
AREA ENLARGED
PHILIPPINES
Makassar Strait
INDIAN OCEAN
EQUATOR
Sunda Strait
I N D O N E S I A
0 mi 1,000
0 km 1,000
Lombok Strait
AUSTRALIA

0 mi 50
0 km 50

VIEWING Blackbeard's Cannons

Before You Watch

A. Discussion. What do you remember from this unit about the pirate Blackbeard? Look back and check your answers.

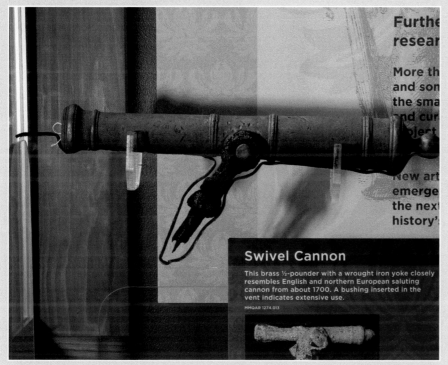

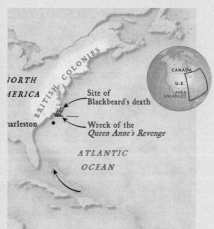

< Objects brought up from a site off the Carolina coast include this 18th-century ship's cannon.

B. Discussion. Why do you think archeologists are interested in the object in the picture?

While You Watch

A. Completion. Complete these sentences by circling the correct word or phrase in each pair.

1. Blackbeard's ship disappeared in (**1717 / 1718**).

2. Blackbeard renamed the ship he stole (*Concorde / Queen Anne's Revenge*).

3. Archeologists hope to find a (**name / date**) on the cannon.

4. Everything that archeologists found on the ship is dated (**before / after**) 1718.

B. Summary. Complete the summary outline of the video using the list of words.

Carolina	300	dirty	X-rays	cannons
water	Goals	1717	salt	1718

1. The *Queen Anne's Revenge*
   A. Captured in _____
   B. French slave ship
   C. Disappeared in _____

2. Shipwreck
   A. Location
      - a kilometer off coast of _____
   B. Findings
      - wooden body gone but _____ still there

3. Cannons
   A. Condition
      - _____ and strange looking
      - _____ years under _____
   B. Cleaning
      - use _____ to see inside
      - remove rocks and put into bath to take off _____

4. _____
   A. finish by 2018
   B. confirm whether it's *Queen Anne's Revenge* or not

After You Watch

Critical Thinking. Discuss these questions with a partner.

1. From the information in this video, is it certain that this is Blackbeard's ship? What evidence supports this theory?

2. What should happen to all of the objects found on the ship?

12

VANISHED!

Pilot Amelia Earhart, photographed in 1931, six years before her mysterious disappearance

Warm Up

Discuss these questions with a partner.

1. What are some of the most dangerous places to visit in the world?

2. Do you know any famous explorers who visited these places?

3. Do you know any famous people who vanished (went missing) or died mysteriously?

Before You Read

A. Completion. What do you know about Mount Everest? Complete the information with answers from the box. One answer is extra.

| 8,850 | 1953 | oxygen | India | 200 | Nepal | cold | 4 |

Everest—known in Tibetan as *Chomolungma*—is the world's highest mountain.

- *Everest's height:* **1.** _____ meters (29,035 feet); each year, it rises by another **2.** _____ millimeters.

- *First people to reach the summit of Everest:* Tenzing Norgay (a Sherpa from **3.** _____) and Edmund Hillary (from New Zealand), in **4.** _____.

- *Health risks:* Because of the extreme **5.** _____, climbers can get frostbite, especially on their fingers and toes.

- *Equipment:* Most Everest climbers carry **6.** _____ tanks to help them breathe.

- *Number of deaths on Everest:* more than **7.** _____, mostly due to avalanches (large amounts of snow falling down the mountain).

B. Predict. Look at the title and read the first paragraph on the next page. What do you think the reading will be about? Read to check your predictions.

MYSTERY ON EVEREST

1   Were Edmund Hillary and Tenzing Norgay really the first
people to reach the top of Mount Everest? Some believe
British climbers George Mallory and Andrew Irvine reached
the summit before them in June 1924. Unfortunately, this is
5   hard to **prove** because both men vanished on the mountain.

1 If you **solve** a problem, you find an answer to it.

A Body in the Snow

In 1999, a team of climbers visited Everest, hoping to solve[1]
this mystery. Near Everest's First Step, on the way to the
summit, the team found Mallory's oxygen tank—**evidence**
10   that he and Irvine were near the top. Close by, a member of
the team, Conrad Anker, discovered Mallory's body.

In addition, when the team examined Mallory's body, they
found items like a knife and matches, but no photos. Why
is this **significant**? Mallory carried a photo of his wife
15   with him. He planned to leave it at the top of Everest, if he
reached the summit.

First to the Top?

Did Mallory and Irvine **achieve** their goal and reach the top? Probably not, says Anker. Here's why:

20 **Difficult path/Poor equipment:** Mallory and Irvine were last seen near Everest's Second Step. This is a 27-meter (90-foot) wall of rock. Climbing this **section** of Everest is extremely difficult, even with modern climbing equipment. Without the right tools, it is **doubtful** Mallory and Irvine were able to **proceed** to the top.

25 **No frostbite:** Mallory and Irvine were near the summit late in the day. Climbers who reach the summit at this time need to camp at the top. If you do this, it is common to **suffer** from frostbite. But Mallory's body had no sign of frostbite.

So what happened to Mallory and Irvine? Anker thinks they
30 probably turned back just after the First Step. When Mallory was going down, perhaps he accidentally fell. Irvine's body has never been found. **Whatever** happened, they will always be remembered as early Everest heroes.[2]

George Mallory photographed in 1909

2 A **hero** is a brave person, someone who does something great.

The frozen remains of Mallory's body were discovered in 1999.

Reading Comprehension

Multiple Choice. Choose the best answer for each question.

Gist

1. The reading is mainly about two climbers who _____.
   a. solved a mystery about Everest
   b. vanished on Everest
   c. recreated Hillary and Norgay's climb
   d. invented new climbing tools

Detail

2. Which statement is true?
   a. Mallory's body showed signs of frostbite.
   b. Conrad Anker's team found two bodies on Everest.
   c. Mallory and Irvine were near the top of Everest in the morning.
   d. Anker's team found some of Mallory's items on the mountain.

Purpose

3. The purpose of the second and third paragraphs is to give reasons why _____.
   a. Mallory may have reached the top
   b. Mallory probably didn't reach the top
   c. Mallory brought an oxygen tank
   d. the body was not Mallory's

Reference

4. In line 15, what does *it* refer to?
   a. the body
   b. the oxygen tank
   c. the summit
   d. the picture

Detail

5. Where were Mallory and Irvine last seen?
   a. at a camp near the bottom of the mountain
   b. at the top of Everest
   c. just below the First Step
   d. just below the Second Step

Vocabulary

6. If Mallory and Irvine *turned back* (line 30), they _____ the mountain.
   a. stopped and went down
   b. went around
   c. tried to walk up
   d. stayed in one place on

Did You Know?

Mallory took a camera like this on his climb. Finding the camera could confirm whether Mallory and Irvine reached the top of Everest; however, the camera has never been found.

Inference

7. Which statement would Conrad Anker probably agree with?
   a. Mallory and Irvine definitely reached the top of Everest.
   b. Mallory and Irvine never got close to the summit.
   c. Mallory and Irvine got close, but didn't reach the top.
   d. Irvine probably reached the top, but not Mallory.

Arguing For and Against a Topic

Writers sometimes present two sides of an argument—giving reasons for and against an idea. Sometimes they list all the reasons *for* first, followed by the reasons *against*. To introduce the reasons, writers may use phrases such as *one reason is . . .* , *in addition . . .* To evaluate a writer's arguments, it can be useful to list the reasons for and against in two columns, like in a T-chart.

A. Scanning. Look back at the reading on pages 163–164. Find and underline evidence that suggests Mallory and Irvine reached the top of Everest, and then circle the reasons against this being true.

B. For and Against. Complete the chart with words from the reading.

Did Mallory and Irvine reach the top of Everest?

Reasons for	Reasons against
Anker's team discovered Mallory's **1.** _____ tank & **2.** _____ near First Step. Team didn't find a(n) **3.** _____ of Mallory's wife. He planned to **4.** _____ it at the summit.	Climbing Everest's Second Step is very **5.** _____, and Mallory and Irvine did not have modern **6.** _____. Mallory's body had no **7.** _____. It is common for people to suffer from this if they **8.** _____ near the summit for the night.

Critical Thinking Discuss with a partner. Based on the evidence in the reading, do you think Mallory and Irvine reached the top of Everest? Why or why not?

Vocabulary Practice

A. Completion. Complete the information with the correct form of words from the box. One word is extra.

| achieve | doubtful | path | prove | significant | suffer |

Tenzing Norgay and Edmund Hillary reached the summit of Everest in 1953. But there have been other **1.** _____ "firsts." On May 25, 2001, blind American climber Erik Weihenmeyer reached Everest's summit. With this **2.** _____, Weihenmeyer **3.** _____ it is possible for people who cannot see to climb the world's highest mountain. Three years later, he climbed Everest again with a group of blind teenagers from Tibet. The **4.** _____ to the top of Lhakpa Ri (one of Everest's summits) was difficult. Because of lack of oxygen, some teens **5.** _____ from extreme headaches. Their amazing journey became a movie called *Blindsight*.

B. Words in Context. Complete each sentence with the correct answer.

1. An example of **evidence** at a crime scene is a _____.

   a. dead body   b. police officer

2. A newspaper has different **sections**. This means it has different _____.

   a. colors   b. parts

3. If you **proceed** in a direction, you _____.

   a. continue in that direction   b. avoid that direction

4. If you can buy **whatever** you want, you can buy _____.

   a. anything   b. only certain things

5. If you are **doubtful** about something, you are _____ about it.

   a. certain   b. uncertain

⌄ Erik Weihenmeyer became the first blind man to reach the summit of Everest.

Word Link We can add **-ever** (meaning *any* or *every*) to certain question words (*who, what, where, when*) to form new words. For example, *whenever* means "at any time."

Before You Read

^ Amelia Earhart in front of her bi-plane named "Friendship" on the island of Newfoundland, Canada

A. Scanning. Read the timeline of Amelia Earhart's life. What record did she break?

Amelia Earhart (*1897–1937*)

1918: Sees a small airplane take off in the snow of Toronto, Canada. Decides she wants to fly.

1921: Becomes a pilot at age 24.

1932: Breaks a world record: is the first woman to fly a plane alone across the Atlantic Ocean.

1937, May–June: Plans to be the first woman to fly a plane around the world. Flies with guide Fred Noonan across the U.S., south to Brazil, and across Africa, Asia, and Australia.

1937, June 29: Earhart and Noonan arrive in New Guinea.

1937, July 2: They take off again, heading for an island in the Pacific Ocean. They are never seen again . . .

B. Predict. What do you think happened to Earhart and Noonan? Read the passage to check your ideas.

THE MISSING PILOT

Howland Island

1 On July 2, 1937, Amelia Earhart and Fred Noonan left New Guinea for Howland Island in the Pacific. This was the longest and most dangerous part of their trip around the world. Earhart had trouble shortly after takeoff. The weather was stormy, so she had to fly
5 at 3,000 meters (10,000 feet). Going this high, the plane used up gas quickly.

After about twenty hours, Earhart and Noonan **approached** Howland Island. The island was only about 105 kilometers (65 miles) away, but the **bright** sun was **shining** in their faces, so
10 they couldn't see it. Near Howland, a ship, the *Itasca*, was waiting. Earhart contacted the ship: "Gas is low," she said. The *Itasca* tried to maintain contact with her, but it got no **response**. Finally, the *Itasca* called for help. People searched for Earhart and Noonan for days. Despite great **efforts**, they found nothing.

15 ## Answers to a Mystery?

What happened to Amelia Earhart? No one knows for sure. During the **flight**, she probably **headed** in the wrong direction because the sun was bright and it was hard to see. Perhaps she got lost; soon after, her plane ran out of gas and she died at sea. Another idea is
20 that she survived the plane **crash**, swam to an uninhabited[1] island, and later died there. A more extreme theory is that she survived the crash and secretly returned to the U.S. with a new identity.

The first theory seems most likely. However, none of these ideas has been proven. Today, people are still **investigating** Earhart's
25 and Noonan's **disappearance** (Noonan's body has also never been found). Whatever happened, Earhart probably died as she wished. "When I go," she said, "I'd like best to go in my plane."

"Women must try to do things as men have tried. When they fail, their failure must be but a challenge to others."

Amelia Earhart

---

1 If a place is **uninhabited**, it has no people.

Reading Comprehension

Multiple Choice. Choose the best answer for each question.

Gist

1. Another title for this reading could be _____.
- a. Pilot Mystery Is Finally Solved
- b. Amelia Earhart Breaks Another Record
- c. What Happened to Amelia Earhart?
- d. The First Female Pilot in the U.S.A.

Detail

2. Why was flying to Howland Island difficult?
- a. Earhart was sick.
- b. Noonan didn't have a map.
- c. Their plane was damaged.
- d. It was very far from New Guinea.

Detail

3. Shortly after taking off from New Guinea, what happened?
- a. Earhart's plane ran out of gas.
- b. There was a bad storm.
- c. Fred Noonan died.
- d. Earhart's plane crashed.

Sequence

4. What happened after Earhart contacted the *Itasca* and before people started searching for her?
- a. She asked for more gas.
- b. The *Itasca* spoke with Earhart.
- c. She tried to land on the *Itasca*.
- d. The *Itasca* called for help.

Vocabulary

5. Which of these words or phrases is most similar in meaning to *ran out of* in line 19?
- a. removed
- b. filled up with
- c. had no more of
- d. caught on fire from

Did You Know?

This jar of face cream was found on a remote Nikumaroro Island site. Experts believe it belonged to Amelia Earhart.

Inference

6. In line 27, when Earhart says "*When I go . . . ,*" what does *go* mean?
- a. fly
- b. die
- c. leave
- d. live

Inference

7. Which statement would the writer of the passage agree with?
- a. Earhart's plane probably ran out of gas and she died at sea.
- b. It is possible that Noonan killed Earhart.
- c. Earhart probably died on an island in the Pacific.
- d. Earhart and Noonan might still be alive today.

Identifying Transition Words

Writers use transition words to add or contrast information. Identifying transition words will help you connect one idea to another.

Adding information

The sun was bright, **and** *it was hard to see.*

The sun was bright. In **addition***, it was hard to see.*

The sun was bright. It was **also** *hard to see.*

Contrasting information

The Itasca *tried to contact her,* **but** *it got no response.*

The Itasca *tried to contact her.* **However***, it got no response.*

The Itasca *tried to contact her. It got no response,* **though***.*

A. Multiple Choice. Read these sentences about Amelia Earhart. Circle the correct word.

1. She studied auto repair in college. (**However / Though**), she changed her focus and later studied medicine.

2. She began taking flying lessons in 1921 (**and / in addition**) later that year bought her first plane.

3. She borrowed money from her family for the plane. She (**and / also**) used the money she earned as a telephone operator.

B. Completion. Complete the summary of Amelia Earhart's disappearance with the phrases in the box (a–e). One phrase is extra.

---

a. and she had to fly very high

b. but they weren't able to stay in contact

c. The search team found nothing, though

d. In addition, it was shining in her eyes

e. However, she never made it there

Amelia Earhart left New Guinea for Howland Island on July 2, 1937. **1.** _____. After takeoff, there was a storm, **2.** _____. After 20 hours of flying, she approached Howland Island. She called the ship Itasca to say gas was low, **3.** _____. The ship called for help, and a search was begun. **4.** _____.

Critical Thinking Discuss with a partner. Do you think we will ever find out what happened to Earhart? Why or why not?

Vocabulary Practice

A. Completion. Complete the information by circling the correct word in each pair.

Jim Thompson was an American businessman who helped revive Thailand's silk industry in the 1950s and 1960s. On March 26, 1967, Thompson **1. (maintained / headed)** out alone for an afternoon walk in Malaysia's Cameron Highlands, and was never seen again. A huge search **2. (approach / effort)** involved more than 400 people spreading out into the jungle, but nothing was found. After a(n) **3. (investigation / flight)**, the conclusion was that he fell into an animal trap or was eaten by a tiger. However, other ideas have been put forward to explain Thompson's **4. (disappearance / response)**. Some believe he was murdered, while others think he faked his own death. His disappearance may always remain a mystery. However, Jim Thompson's presence can still be felt. Shoppers crowd his stores in Thailand to buy **5. (shine / bright)** scarves and elegant ties. His former home in Bangkok remains one of the capital's top tourist attractions.

^ The last photo taken of Jim Thompson before he disappeared in Malaysia in 1967

B. Words in Context. Complete each sentence with the correct answer.

1. Something that **shines** is _____.

   a. bright   b. dull

2. If there is a plane **crash**, a plane _____.

   a. hits the ground hard   b. takes off quickly

3. A person who is going to take a **flight** needs to go to the _____.

   a. airport   b. train station

4. When you **approach** something, you _____ it.

   a. get closer to   b. walk away from

5. A **response** is a(n) _____.

   a. plan or need   b. answer or reply

> **Word Link** We can add **dis-** to some words to show an opposite meaning. For example, if something *disappears*, you can no longer see it. If you *dislike* someone, you don't like them.

VIEWING Earhart Mystery

Before You Watch

A. Matching. You will hear these words in the video. Match them to their definitions. Then add them to the photo captions below.

1. spy •   • a. the feeling that you need to drink something

2. reef •   • b. a long line of rocks, the top of which is just below or above the sea

3. thirst •   • c. a person who tries to find out secret information

B. Discussion. The pictures and captions below show different possibilities of what happened to Earhart. Which is least likely? Which is most likely?

While You Watch

A. Sequencing. Number the theories below from 1 to 4 in the order they appear in the video.

Earhart landed on a(n) _____, swam to shore, but later died of _____.

Earhart went to the Marshall Islands to _____ on the Japanese.

Earhart landed near Howland Island, where her plane sank in the ocean.

Earhart didn't die at sea but returned to the U.S. under a different name.

B. Completion. Complete the word web about the video. Use words from the box. Two words are extra.

captured	different	housewife	reason	swam
died	gas	ocean	spy	time

- flew toward Howland Island
- ran out of **1.** _____
- landed in the **2.** _____
- boat sank

- flew to a(n) **3.** _____ island
- landed on reef and then went to island
- died of thirst

What happened to Amelia Earhart?

- returned to U.S.
- lived as a(n) **8.** _____
- new name: Irene Bolam

- flew to Marshall Islands
- **4.** _____ by Japanese
- **5.** _____ there

- American **6.** _____
- flew to Marshall Islands
- gave U.S. Navy **7.** _____ to go there

After You Watch

Critical Thinking. Discuss these questions with a partner.

1. After viewing the video, what do you think probably happened to Amelia Earhart?
2. Have any of your ideas about Earhart changed from watching the video?
3. Is it important that we find out what happened to Earhart? Why or why not?

Photo Credits

1 O. Louis Mazzatenta/NGC, 3, 17 (cr) Dan Callister/Alamy, 4–5, 91 (c) Ralph Lee Hopkins/NGC, 7 Frans Lanting/NGC, 8–9 (t) Mauricio Handler/NGC, 10 (tr) Bill Curtsinger/NGC, 10 (b), 11 (t), 12–13 (t) Ralph Lee Hopkins/NGC, 11 (br) Frans Lanting/NGC, 12 (br) Frans Lanting/NGC, 13 (cr) Joel Sartore/NGC, 14, 18 (t) Paula Bronstein/Getty Images, 15 (br), 16–17 (t) William Albert Allard/NGC, 16 (cr) Gilbert M. Grosvenor/NGC, 18 (b) NOVICA, 19 (c) Cyril Ruoso/JH Editorial/Minden Pictures/Getty Images, 20 (br) Cyril Ruoso/JH Editorial/Minden Pictures/Getty Images, 21, 25, 26–27 (t) Bill Hatcher/NGC, 23 Gregg Bleakney/RibbonofRoad.com, 24 Jason Edwards/NGC, 25 (cr) Design Pics Inc/NGC, 27 (cr) James P. Blair/NGC, 28 Ulla Lohmann /NGC, 30–31 Ulla Lohmann/NGC, 30 (cr) cbpix/Alamy, 31 (tr) JS Callahan/tropicalpix/Alamy, 32 Tino Soriano/NGC, 33, 47, 48, 76, 92, 106, 118, 131, 132, 146, 173 National Geographic, 34 (cr) Raul Touzon/NGC, 35, 40–41, 44–45 Fin Costello/Getty Images, 36–37, 39 (t) Kyle Gustafson/For The Washington Post/Getty Images, 38 Finbarr O'Reilly/Senegal-Music/Reuters, 39 (cr) Pressmaster/Shutterstock.com, 42 (t) Maggie Steber/NGC, 42 (br) Anna Tsekhmister/Shutterstock.com, 44 (cr) RodrigoBlanco/iStockphoto.com, 46 (t) Aleksandar Todorovic/Shutterstock.com, 46 (b) Chris McGrath/Getty Images, 49 NASA Images, 50–51, 53, 54–55 ESA and NASA/NGC, 52 Dana Berry/NGC, 53 (cr) NASA Images, 55 (b) Kenny Tong, 56, 58–59, 60 Mars One/EyePress EPN/Newscom, 57 NASA Images/NGC, 58 Jeanne Modderman and Rebecca Hale/NGC, NASA/NGC, 60 (br) NASA/NGC, 61 (cr) Time Life Pictures/Contributor/Time & Life Pictures Getty Images, 61 (bl) NASA Images, 63 Mike Theiss/NGC, 64–65 (t) John Tomanio/NGC, 66, 67, 68–69 Panoramic Images/NGC, 67 (cr) Ira Block/NGC, 69 (tr) Richard Nowitz/NGC, 70–71, 72–73, 74 Mike Theiss/NGC, 72 (cr) Yasuyoshi Chiba/AFP/Getty Images, 74 Peeter Viisimaa/The Image Bank/Getty Images, 75 (r) Kayla A/Shutterstock.com, 77 Power and Syred/Science Source, 78–79, 80, 81 (br), 82, 83, 84 (t) David Liittschwager/NGC, 82 (br) Maxim Ibragimov/Shutterstock.com, 83 Michael Nichols/NGC, 84 S.E. Thorpe, 85, 88–89, 90 Science Photo Library-SCIEPRO/Brand X Pictures/Getty Images, 86–87 (b) Lawson Parker/NGC, 88 (cr) Science Photo Library-KTSDesign/Brand X Pictures/Getty Images, 89 (br) Brian Gordon Green/NGC, 93 Will Van Overbeek/NGC, 94 Raul Martin/NGC, 95 Pixeldust Studios/NGC, 96 Alice Mary Herden/Shutterstock.com, 97 (cr) Leonello Calvetti/Shutterstock.com, 97 (t) In Green/Shutterstock.com, 98–99 (t) Brandelet/Shutterstock.com, 99 (b) Matte FX, Matte FX Inc/NGC, 100–101 (t) Ira Block/NGC, 100 (tr) Pixeldust Studios/NGC, 100 (cr) Pixel Dust Studios/NGC, 102–103 (t) Pichugin Dmitry/Shutterstock.com, 102 (cr) Ira Block/NGC, 104 (t) majeczka/Shutterstock.com, 104 (br) John Sibbick/NGC, 105 Alexal/Shutterstock.com, 107 Charles Bowman/Getty Images, 108–109 Warner Bros/The Kobal Collection, 109 DNY59/iStockphoto.com, 110–111, 114–115, 116 (t) andreiuc88/Shutterstock.com, 111 akg-images/Newscom, 112–113 Proehl Proehl/Picture Press/Getty Images, 114 (cr) ICHIRO/Getty Images, 116 (cr) Eric Fowke/Alamy, 117 DC/Art Resource, NY, 119 Michael Nichols/NGC, 120–121 (t) Chelyabinsk.ru, Yekaterina Pustynnikova/AP Images, 121 (cr) Courtesy of Michael Farmer, 122 Thomas J. Abercrombie/NGC, 123 (cr) Jonathan Blair/Corbis, 123, 124–125 (t) Pavel Vakhrushev/Shutterstock.com, 125 (cr) Africa Studio/Shutterstock.com, 126, 128, 129, 130 (t) Frans Lanting/NGC, 127 (br) Shebeko/Shutterstock.com, 128 (br) Mark Thiessen/NGC, 131 (c) Mark Thiessen/NGC, 133 O. Louis Mazzatenta/NGC, 134–135 (t) Pure Rendereing GMBH/NGC, 136 (b) O. Louis Mazzatenta/NGC, 137, 138–139 (t) Asliuzunoglu/Shutterstock.com, 137 (cr) Pure Rendereing GMBH/NGC, 139 (b) Ira Block/NGC, 140 (t) Kenneth Garrett/NGC, 142 (cr), 142–143, 144 (t), 144 (cr) Kenneth Garrett/NGC, 145 Kenneth Garrett//NGC, 147 Wes C. Skiles/NGC, 148–149 Cliff Wassmann/E+/Getty Images, 150 N.C. Wyeth/NGC, 151 (cr) Nick Kaloterakis/NGC, 153 (br) Kathryn Scott Osler/The Denver Post/Getty Images, 154 Walt Disney Pictures/Mountain, Peter/Album/Newscom, 155 Apic/Getty Images, 156 Raleigh News & Observer/McClatchy-Tribune/Getty Images, 156–157, 158 (t) Kuttelvaserova Stuchelova/Shutterstock.com, 159 Rebecca Hale/NGC, 161 Mark Owen/Blackout Concepts/Alamy, 162–163 (t) MJ Photography/Alamy, 164 (tr) AFP/Getty Images, 164 (b) Aurora Photos/Alamy, 165 (t) Alex Treadway/NGC, 165 (cr) Mark Thiessen/NGC, 166–167 (t) Igor Plotnikov/Shutterstock.com, 167 (br) Didrik Johnck/Corbis, 168 Getty Images, 170–171 (t) KKulikov/Shutterstock.com, 170 (cr) Tighar/Barcroft USA/Barcoft Media/Getty Images, 172 (t) Irina_QQQ/Shutterstock.com, 172 (cr) Nik Wheeler/Alamy

NGC = National Geographic Creative

Illustration Credits

15, 22, 26, 29, 38, 45, 68, 71, 105, 108, 111, 128, 140, 158, 159, 162, 169 National Geographic Maps

Text Credits

9 Adapted from "Ten Cool Things About Dolphins," by George David Gordon: NGK, Jun/Jul 2005, and "The Secret Language of Dolphins," by Crispin Boyer: NGK, Jun/Jul 2007, 15 Adapted from "Thailand's Urban Giants," by Douglas H. Chadwick: NGM, Oct 2005, 23 Adapted from "Your Story: Living the Dream," by Gregg Bleakney: NGA, Dec 2006/Jan 2007, 29 Adapted from "Extreme Destination: Yasur Volcano, Vanuatu," by Ted Allen: NGA, Winter 1999, 37 Adapted from "Hip-Hop Planet," by James McBride: NGM, Apr 2007, 43 Adapted from "Making Music Boosts Brain's Language Skills," by Victoria Jaggard: NGN, 51 Adapted from "Alien Life: Astronomers Predict Contact by 2025," by Hillary Mayell: NGN, Nov 14, 2003, and "Aliens 'Absolutely' Exist, SETI Astronomer Believes," by Tom Foreman: NGN, Apr 1, 2003, 57 Adapted from "Space: The Next Generation," by Guy Gugliotta: NGM, Oct 2007, and "Q & A with Robert Zubrin," by Ted Chamberlain: NGA, Sep/Oct 2000, 65 Adapted from "The Most Influential Cities," by Luna Shyr: NGM, Dec 2011, 71 Adapted from "Playing Rio," by Antonio Regalado: NGM, Oct 2012, 79 Adapted from "Within One Cubic Foot," by Edward O. Wilson: NGM, Feb 2010, 85 Adapted from "Small, Small World," by Nathan Wolfe: NGM, Jan 2013, 95 Adapted from "New Picture of Dinosaurs Is Emerging," by Hillary Mayell: NGN, Dec 17, 2002, and "Flesh and Bone," by Joel Achenbach: NGM, Mar 2003, 101 Adapted from "Extreme Dinosaurs," by John Updike: NGM, Dec 2007, 108 Adapted from "Guardians of the Fairy Tale," by Thomas O'Neill: NGM, Dec 1999, 113 Adapted from "The Seven Ravens,": http://www.nationalgeographic.com/grimm/index2.html, 121 Adapted from "Meet the Meteorite Hunter," by Jeremy Berlin: NGN, Feb 16, 2013, 127 Adapted from "Russian Smokejumpers," by Glenn Hodges: NGM, Aug 2002, 135 Adapted from "Terra-Cotta Army: True Colors," by Brook Larmer: NGM, June 2012, 141 Adapted from "The Pyramid Builders," by Virginia Morell: NGM, Nov 2001, 149 Adapted from "Grim Life Cursed Real Pirates of Caribbean," by Stefan Lovgren: NGN, Jul 11, 2003, and "Pirates of the Whydah," by Donovan Webster: NGM, May 1999, 155 Adapted from "Pirates!": http://www.nationalgeographic.com/pirates/adventure.html, 163 Adapted from "Mystery on Everest," by Conrad Anker: NGM, Oct 1999, and "Out of Thin Air," by David Roberts: NGA, Fall 1999, 137 Adapted from "Amelia Earhart," by Virginia Morell: NGM, Jan 1998, and "Expedition Scours Pacific for Amelia Earhart Wreck," by Jennifer Hile: NGN, Dec 15, 2003

NGC = National Geographic Creative
NGK = National Geographic Kids
NGM = National Geographic Magazine
NGA = National Geographic Adventure
NGN = National Geographic News (http://news.nationalgeographic.com/news)

Acknowledgments

The Authors and Publisher would like to thank the following teaching professionals for their valuable feedback during the development of this series:

Ahmed Mohamed Motala, University of Sharjah; **Ana Laura Gandini**, Richard Anderson School; **Andrew T. Om**, YBM PINE R&D; **Dr. Asmaa Awad**, University of Sharjah; **Atsuko Takase**, Kinki University, Osaka; **Bogdan Pavliy**, Toyama University of International Studies; **Brigitte Maronde**, Harold Washington College, Chicago; **Bunleap Heap**, American Intercon Institute; **Carey Bray**, Columbus State University; **Carmella Lieske**, Shimane University; **Chanmakara Hok**, American Intercon Institute; **Choppie Tsann Tsang Yang**, National Taipei University; **Cynthia Ross**, State College of Florida; **David Schneer**, ACS International, Singapore; **Dawn Shimura**, St. Norbert College; **David Barrett**, Goldenwest College, CA; **Dax Thomas**, Keio University; **Deborah E. Wilson**, American University of Sharjah; **Elizabeth Rodacker**, Bakersfield College; **Emma Tamaianu-Morita**, Akita University; **Fu-Dong Chiou**, National Taiwan University; **Gavin Young**, Iwate University; **George Galamba**, Woodland Community College; **Gigi Santos**, American Intercon Institute; **Gursharan Kandola**, Language and Culture Center, University of Houston, TX; **Heidi Bundschoks**, ITESM, Sinaloa Mexico; **Helen E. Roland**, ESL/FL Miami-Dade College-Kendall Campus; **Hiroyo Yoshida**, Toyo University; **Hisayo Murase**, Doshisha Women's College of Liberal Arts; **Ikuko Kashiwabara**, Osaka Electro-Communication University; **J. Lorne Spry**, Contracting University Lecturer; **Jamie Ahn**, English Coach, Seoul; **Jane Bergmann**, The University of Texas at San Antonio; **Jennie Farnell**, University of Connecticut; **José Olavo de Amorim**, Colegio Bandeirantes, Sao Paulo; **Kyoungnam Shon**, Avalon English; **Luningning C. Landingin**, American Intercon Institute; **Mae-Ran Park**, Pukyong National University, Busan; **Mai Minh Tiên**, Vietnam Australia International School; **Marina Gonzalez**, Instituto Universitario de Lenguas Modernas Pte., Buenos Aires; **Mark Rau**, American River College, Sacramento CA; **Max Heineck**, Academic Coordinator/Lecturer, King Fahd University of Petroleum & Minerals; **Dr. Melanie Gobert**, Higher Colleges of Technology; **Michael C. Cheng**, National Chengchi University; **Michael Johnson**, Muroran Institute of Technology; **Michael McGuire**, Kansai Gaidai University; **Muriel Fujii**, University of Hawaii; **Patrick Kiernan**, Meiji University; **Philip Suthons**, Aichi Shukutoku University; **Renata Bobakova**, English Programs for Internationals, Columbia, SC; **Rhonda Tolhurst**, Kanazawa University; **Rodney Johnson**, Kansai Gaidai University; **Rosa Enilda Vásquez Fernandez**, John F. Kennedy Institute of Languages, Inc.; **Sandra Kern**, New Teacher Coach, School District of Philadelphia; **Shaofang Wu**, National Cheng Kung University; **Sovathey Tim**, American Intercon Institute; **Stephen Shrader**, Notre Dame Seishin Women's University; **Sudeepa Gulati**, Long Beach City College; **Susan Orias**, Broward College; **Thays Ladosky**, Colegio Damas, Recife; **Thea Chan**, American Intercon Institute; **Tom Justice**, North Shore Community College; **Tony J.C. Carnerie**, UCSD English Language Institute; **Tsung-Yuan Hsiao**, National Taiwan Ocean University, Keelung; **Virginia Christopher**, University of Calgary-Qatar; **Vuthy Lorn**, American Intercon Institute; **Wm Troy Tucker**, Edison State College; **Yohei Murayama**, Kagoshima University; **Yoko Sakurai**, Aichi University; **Yoko Sato**, Tokyo University of Agriculture and Technology